TIGER

BABIES

STRIKE BACK

Also by Kim Wong Keltner

I Want Candy
Buddha Baby
The Dim Sum of All Things

TIGER
BABIES
STRIKE BACK

How I Was Raised by a Tiger Mom but
Could Not Be Turned to the Dark Side

KIM WONG KELTNER

wm
WILLIAM MORROW
An Imprint of HarperCollins*Publishers*

Grateful acknowledgment is made to reprint portions of "The Slow Boob Movement." Reprinted with permission from *The Bigger the Better, the Tighter the Sweater*, edited by Lisa Taggart and Samantha Schoech, published by Seal Press, 2007.

The names and identifying characteristics of some of the individuals featured throughout this book have been changed to protect their privacy.

HarperCollins books may be purchased for educational, business, or sales promotional use. For information please write: Special Markets Department, HarperCollins Publishers, 10 East 53rd Street, New York, NY 10022.

Library of Congress Cataloging-in-Publication Data has been applied for.

ISBN 978-0-06-222929-8

13 14 15 16 17   OV/RRD   10 9 8 7 6 5 4 3 2 1

For Lucy

Contents

Acknowledgments

Big thanks to my editor, Erika Tsang, whose great ideas, tact, and finesse helped me so much. With her insightful suggestions, Erika prompted me to find what I most wanted to convey in this book, and she did it without making me cry. That's saying a lot because I shed tears easily, like at the end of *Return of the Jedi*, when that one Ewok doesn't wake up.

Thanks to my agent, Agnes Birnbaum, at Bleecker Street Associates, for always being in my corner and believing in this project from the beginning.

Thanks also to Rolf Keltner for early proofreading and letting me include anecdotes about him in this book.

And, of course, much gratitude to my mother. At one point, I said, "Mom, you know how every book has to have a villain? Well, in this one it's gonna hafta be you." She thought for a moment, and then just said, "OK." So thanks, Mom, for being strong enough to respond that way. In addition, a big hug goes out to my dad. I appreciate both of you allowing me the freedom to share my point of view.

And last, thanks to Lucy Keltner, who is already a brilliant artist and writer at age nine. May we always share hugs and laughs.

TIGER BABIES

STRIKE BACK

PART 1

Here's Where the Fun Begins

1

Tiger Babies Strike Back

We are the survivors of the tap dance brigade, Chinese school, and interminable piano lessons. We are frustrated by our parents and spending a small fortune on therapy. My Chinese auntie once told me that if I wasn't driving a Mercedes-Benz by the time I turned thirty years old, I'd be a total loser. And even though I'd gotten straight As my whole life, earned a bachelor's degree with a double major at UC Berkeley in four years, worked a full-time job while my husband was in graduate school, wrote three novels before I turned thirty-eight, and am raising one great kid, do you know what my mother thinks of me? She thinks I am lazy.

I am writing this book because I've just returned from vacation with my parents, and the only way I could stand the bickering, silent criticism, and their tiger *vibe* was to sit still in the backseat and pretend I was dead. I pretended I was DEAD.

I sat there and visualized myself floating just outside the car window, out there on the California landscape, floating like a ghost, or a harrier, and tried to find peaceful death while Johnny Mathis crooned on the CD player.

Why? Because this is what happens when you are raised by a Tiger Mother. You get a liberal arts education and use it against her. The *New York Times* speculates that the study of the humanities is obsolete on college campuses. Oh, no. You need the arsenal of history and literature behind you if you're going to take on a Machiavellian Tiger Mom.

For survivors of a Chinese upbringing, turnabout is fair play. The culture of my ancestors made me obedient up to a point, but then my American side couldn't help but want to blow stuff up. I was forced into a life of high academics, Chinese school, and rote memorization of the Five Chinese Classics, but I didn't learn a thing. Well, except how to sneak out at night and have dirty fun somewhere else, away from the watchful eyes of my control-freaky Tiger Parents.

The history of Chinese in America consists of railroad building, tunnel excavating, and gold mining. But that is the story predominantly of Chinese men. Meanwhile, we girls were drowned in wells or sold for a few dollars by our very own parents who didn't seem to care that we'd be auctioned to the highest bidder in the Gold Mountain of San Francisco.

But now we're doctors, lawyers, and CEOs. Nonetheless, no matter how different our personalities or professions are these days, it seems that all anyone wants to know is if we are Tiger Moms. And is it just me, or does the world only want to hear from a woman if she has been deemed *hot*? We've come a long way, baby! From concubines to MILFs in one century.

What does go on inside the Chinese American mind? We'd

better start thinking about it before China takes over the whole world with insane pollution, supertall basketball hunkies, and fake Ming vases selling for millions. Oh, and don't forget that all the little hooks that make up every bra, from Warner's to La Perla, are made in China. American breasts depend on China. Your rack depends on China. And hence, the world depends on understanding us, Chinese American women. We are more than a design on someone's biceps. Our individuality is a chink in the armor of one of the world's largest economies.

We have an interior life that no one can touch. We rule ourselves behind a yellow screen, like the empress dowager ruling China behind a transparent scrim. The world still sees Suzie Wong, but we are many faces at once. We are simultaneously the forgotten girl in the well, an adorable adopted baby, the queen of the Western Palace, the Tiger Mom, the sexy siren, or dominatrix doormat in men's minds, and all the while dutiful daughters, good girls, and faceless sewing women.

Why does a Tiger Mother feel like she has to be one? Maybe because there's an emotional aspect to Chinese American history that our organs are steeped in, like strong tea, but this vital part of our existence goes unexamined and unrecognized. We are the original *Girl with the Dragon Tattoo,* but the tattoo is on our hearts, stitched with an embroidery needle in the forbidden stitch.

Our mothers have raised kids who are more American than Chinese, and we want to lob a Molotov cocktail into the family courtyard so it rolls into the red chamber. Praise Asian nerds and raise the red lantern to comic book geeks, Goth girls, and Ph.D.s who hate Hello Kitty. Our Chinese parents sent us to college, unwittingly giving us the tools to dismantle the family

home, brick by brick, wall by wall, just like the old neighborhoods in Beijing that are being demolished, sold piece by piece
as antiques, relics of an old way, auctioned off for the highest
dollar. We teach our elders how to get on Facebook, and then
we unfriend them.

Please allow me to pull back a velvet curtain and show you
what an American of Chinese descent really thinks about daily
life, motherhood, and navigating the world's misperceptions. I
will hold up this viewfinder just for you, and if you can't deci-
pher some of the Mandarin or Cantonese subtitles, I am happy
to be your American translator.

2

Tiger Mom,
I'm Just Not That into You

If William Blake were alive today and writing parenting books, he might rework the beginning of his famous poem as, "Tyger! Tyger! burning bright / In the *midlife crisis* of the night . . ."

Battle Hymn of the Tiger Mother by Amy Chua was a book that claimed that Chinese parenting is superior to Western ways of child rearing. Pitting Chinese against Caucasians certainly made for dramatic reading. The power play of juxtaposing permissive American moms versus Tiger Mothers amped up everyone's insecurities, and suddenly there was a new dragon lady in town.

But not every Chinese parent rules the home with an iron fist of fury. Tiger Moms might think they're kickin' it old school, but Tiger Babies like me are tired of feeling kicked around. I was raised by a Tiger Mom, and yet I choose to raise my own daughter with more tenderness and hugs than I ever received. I don't believe in threatening children, calling them names, or pushing their limits until they are screaming or in tears.

Why does Chua call herself a Tiger Mother anyway? Because her Chinese zodiac sign is a tiger? All right, if that's how she wants to play it. On that note, a few years ago, when my daughter, Lucy, was six years old, we were at a Chinese restaurant, and she was checking out a placemat with Chinese horoscopes printed on it. Carefully studying the animal pictures with the corresponding dates, she asked me in what year I was born. Tracing her tiny finger over the drawing of the rooster, she looked up with excited eyes and said, "Mommy! Are you a COCK?"

I smiled the awkward, slightly chagrined smile of tired moms everywhere. I did not launch into an explanation of this alternate name for a rooster, which now enjoys more colloquial popularity in pornographic movies. I wanted to affirm her abilities, and not stammer out a definition that would only serve to betray my own hang-ups. I gave her the only logical answer.

"Yes," I said with a straight face. "Mommy is a cock."

Tiger Mother meet Cock Mommy.

Every Asian mother I know has now been asked if she is a Tiger Mom. Our ethnic background alone seems to elicit this question. I always answer no, but maybe the Tiger Mother moniker is attractive to some women who like the idea of not being viewed as pushovers anymore. Being perceived as a Stage 4 stage mom is perhaps preferable after decades—no, centuries—of being seen only as a pretty face.

And Asian women know all about saving face, don't we? But

on playgrounds I've always had my own nickname for these extreme *mompetitors*. I didn't know Tiger Mother is what these ladies wanted to be called. When they turned their backs to adjust the straps on their four-thousand-dollar jog strollers, I'd just say, "Nice wheels." Then just out of earshot, I'd add a piquant "*Bitchface*."

As a child I never knew what dirt felt like on bare feet, and I never once ran through a sprinkler on a hot day. My parents, being Chinese, thought I might catch stupid that way. In contrast, in raising my own child, I want her to focus her attention on having fun. I want her to play. And I don't mean I want her to play piano at Carnegie Hall by the time she turns fourteen. I mean I want her to play. I'm not going to force her into nonstop extracurricular activities and academic supremacy at the cost of having no sleepovers, no friends, and no fun at all. I know that's not very Chinese of me.

Not everybody can be Number One in birth order, academic ability, and physical prowess. I say we need to put the brakes on exalting achievement at the cost of everything else. Kindness, compassion, and friendliness are not second-rate qualities, nor are children who get Bs second-class citizens. All this competition obscures the truth that between cultures and across class lines, we are not enemies. Let's hold each other up, not step on and over each other in pursuit of the false distinction of superiority. Let's open our hands and our hearts because there is no "better than."

Tiger parenting makes lonely fools of us all. Being raised in an environment of intense competition, endless nitpicking, and zero tenderness leaves one suspicious and disoriented, not knowing whom to trust since the place that should have been your hearth and home is more like catfight central.

And now that we're older and a little wiser, we may still never fully feel our parents' approval, get the attention we deserve, or achieve pinnacles of success good enough for their specifications. Even someone who looks like a perfect son or daughter on the outside feels like a square peg in a round hole sometimes. Instead of all of us trying to fit into the confines of a Chinese box, we can rewrite the scripts for our own lives and become whom we want to be.

With our own young children now, what are we to make of our Tiger Mothers? Even if we have been wronged, and if we are still dealing with the consequences of our own strict upbringing, let's put down our imaginary hatchets, sharpened knitting needles, and sidelong glances as cutting as daggers. These days, when my mother still occasionally takes a jab at me, I try to remember Yoda from *The Empire Strikes Back*. He says, "Away put your weapon, I mean you no harm."

That's right, Tiger Mama! I mean you no harm. But still, I've got some stuff I'm gonna say.

To paraphrase Philip Larkin, "They fuck you up, your [Chinese] mum and dad. They may not mean to, but they do."

Tiger Babies, let's strike back. After all, *The* Chinese *Kids Are All Right*.

3

How the Unformed,
Chinese American Blob Takes Shape

In pictures of my mother from the late 1960s, she looked like Betty Draper from *Mad Men*, but Chinese. She wore pearls like Jackie Kennedy, and a little wiglet to fluff out her hairdo. She watched over two little Chinese boys and me, a blob on her lap. My dad was rockin' the pocket protector and short-sleeved, button-down shirt, nerd glasses, and flattop. He was an engineer (natch!) and my mom was a housewife.

When I ask her why we moved to San Francisco, my mom claims she wanted us to have more Chinese culture and be closer to our grandparents, both sets of whom resided in the city. My mother also says she didn't want us playing exclusively with white kids. Okay. So we moved to the City by the Bay, and not long thereafter began Chinese school, tap-dancing class, piano lessons, and many trips into Chinatown even though we lived several miles away, in the Twin Peaks neighborhood.

My mom's parents lived near Chinatown, and I was frequently parked at their apartment. There at Pau Pau and Gung Gung's place is where Chineseness and Americanness really blended. I'd watch *The Brady Bunch* while eating black-vinegared chicken soup, then *Happy Days* with *cha siu bao,* or sticky rice and Chinese sausages while *Leave It to Beaver* was on. And all the while, my grandpa, Gung Gung, would be shouting into the phone, in either Cantonese or Shanghainese, emphasizing his points with the occasional cuss word in English.

My grandparents ran a travel agency in Chinatown, and when I was four, I spent every day there. Behind the main office in a closet-sized room, I sat on a swivel chair at a small table, equipped with colored pencils, paper, crappy mucilage, and a Royal typewriter. Watching over me was a glamour shot of Miss Chinatown 1973, hanging crooked on the wall.

Tours to Hong Kong were being brokered in the front office, but back behind that gold-and-copper-colored curtain, I was left alone and scheming, typing out gibberish words until one day those black letters tap-snapping off that inky ribbon became, before my very eyes, actual sentences. *Tap! Snap!* A funeral motorcade for a Chinatown bigwig would be dolorously passing before the sunlit window, but ghosts couldn't eat me alive when I was typing furiously, a Dixon Ticonderoga between my baby teeth that weren't even loose yet.

At lunchtime, my grandma Lucy would take me across the street to Uncle's Café for sweetened, grass-flavored black gelatin with cream poured over it. Sounds weird, but it was excellent. Then there'd be vanilla ice cream the color of unsalted butter that tasted rich and eggy like custard. Did everything taste better as a kid? Or perhaps the mind was so new and the taste buds not deadened yet, so flavors and coffee smells were just brighter and more pungent, permanently staining my imagination.

Walking down Grant Avenue, we said hello to the residents of Chinatown. They seemed to love my grandma Lucy with her pretty, bouffant hairdo, and Grandpa Lemuel in his brown suit and fedora that made him look like Jimmy Stewart in *Vertigo,* only shorter, and more Chinese. I strolled between them, taking in the sights and sounds, bitter odors and grown-ups' shoes. Where was everybody going so fast? Where had they come from, and why was everyone smiling so brightly, reaching out and clasping my small hand so tightly? They looked in my eyes with such sadness, those adults.

I was a kid wanting something I couldn't describe, wanting to know everything. If I could only get these adults to talk to me, to tell me their stories, I knew it would be like walking through a book, just like Gumby.

But it would take years before even my own relatives would tell me anything. For instance, my grandparents who were walking right beside me with my miniature body between them had a very dramatic story of their own that I would not find out about until many years later.

Gung Gung's name was Lemuel Jen, and he was a Chinese man with distinct American bombast. He came to Angel Island in 1913 at age six with an "uncle" who may or may not have been actually related to him. Lemuel always claimed to have lived in the Spreckels Mansion as a boy, and no one could really refute his story, so for all purposes we believed him. The mansion still sits atop Washington Street in San Francisco, and with its Beaux-Arts grandeur it's easy to imagine a Chinese cook living in the servants' quarters with a little Chinese boy playing underfoot. The white family that owned the house took a liking to my grandpa as a boy, and they especially were concerned with his education. After Galileo High School, Lemuel attended UC Berkeley and George Washington University, assisted financially by his pseudoadoptive white parents. When I asked my relatives more about those early days, the uncle fades from everyone's memory and all that is left is whatever we can glean from two black-and-white photos of my grandpa as a young man, standing between an elderly white couple, everyone smiling and proud.

My grandpa spoke a lot about playing football and being such a fast runner that he was known in school as "Chinese Lightning." When he asked the coach why he was never put in any games, this man whom my grandpa claimed had great fondness for him gave him the news straight. "I wish I could, Lem. But I can't on account of you being Chinese."

After earning a political science degree from George Washington University, my grandpa looked for a job, but encountered much discrimination. So he went back to China in search of work. He was a newspaperman in Shanghai when he met my grandmother. It was the early 1930s and Shanghai was known as the Paris of the East, with colonial-style buildings on the Bund and fancy dance halls. Of course, there also existed extreme poverty and people dying in the streets, but as my mind conjures the family lore, these unsavory truths are expunged. Sticking with the Chinese American fairy tale, Lemuel Jen spotted a young woman named Lucy Chow, thinking she was a rich debutante. My grandmother told me many years later that she was actually wearing a borrowed dress the night she met Gung Gung. Her family had once been rich but her father had been killed fighting for Sun Yat-sen's Republic in the overthrow of the Qing Dynasty. Her mother remarried, to a "fat, old man" who would not have accepted a woman who'd been wed before, so my grandma was forced to pretend she was her mother's niece, not her daughter. Her mother had begged the new husband to allow her niece to work in the house as a maid. My grandma Lucy, Pau Pau, would tell me these things as she nibbled Pepperidge Farm butter cookies in her Russian Hill apartment, over commercials during *Bonanza*.

Eventually my grandpa Lemuel got a job with the U.S. government in the Lend-Lease program. Before the United States officially joined the Allied Forces in World War II, it was "lending" military supplies to other countries and needed people like him to translate and work as liaisons.

In 1949, they left Hong Kong on USS *General Gordon* and landed in San Francisco, my grandpa's adopted hometown. They scrambled for money with odd jobs such as peeling pounds of shrimp for local restaurants, delivering newspapers, and helping out in Chinese-owned grocery stores and curio shops. They eventually started a travel agency on Clay Street in Chinatown. Meanwhile, in addition to my mother and aunt, my grandparents also had five other children. In pictures from those days, Pau Pau looks elegant with her perfectly coiffed hair and tight cheongsams, the Chinese-style dress with a high Mandarin collar, side zipper, and slit up the side. Her style and aplomb combined with Grandpa Lemuel's chutzpah epitomized for me the can-do attitude that propelled them toward the American Dream.

And that was how I came to be walking down Grant Avenue with them as a wide-eyed four-year-old. I felt safe with them.

At the time, I was just a content little kid, and surrounded in the ethnic cocoon that was Chinatown, I made no distinction between myself and the other Chinese I saw around me. After that year with my grandparents, I started kindergarten and didn't go to their office as often, but throughout my childhood, I still visited Chinatown every Saturday morning. My parents would help Gung Gung and Pau Pau with travel agency work, and my brothers and I would goof around on the streets, hanging around our cousin's grandpa's grocery store. It was the first market in Chinatown to carry both Chinese and American products, so you could get your dried cuttlefish and Cap'n Crunch all in one stop. We would run in the aisles as Yeh Yeh watched us bemusedly in his greengrocer's apron.

My brothers and I were American kids for most of the week, Chinese kids on Saturdays. We were Chinese Kids Lite. We ran around Chinatown like a Spanky and Our Gang cluster of urban urchins, and while my brothers and cousin went to Joe Jung's or Jackson Café for French fries, I ran off to my tap-dancing lesson at the YMCA with Tony Wing.

As the years went by and I grew from five years old to ten, I incrementally began to notice differences between other kids in Chinatown and me. Their hand-knit and dollar-store clothes looked weird to me (not that my I'M WITH STUPID T-shirt and tube socks were the height of fashion either), and their haltingly spoken, heavily accented English—that is, when they weren't speaking in Chinese—was something I found exasperating.

And I was equally foreign to them as well. If I encountered girls my age, we eyeballed each other warily, taking in all the visual cues that might tell us who was American-born and who was fresh-off-the-boat. If I said "Hello" to a girl and didn't get a reply, I knew she didn't speak English, and if she said something in Cantonese and I remained mute, it was sufficient proof that I didn't speak Chinese. Our faces may have looked similar, but we had nothing further to say to each other.

Somehow, looking alike but having nothing in common made us instant enemies. The standoff between other little girls and me was proof that animosity within the Chinese population could start from an early age. An us-versus-them mentality between assimilated and immigrant groups simmered within all Chinatown. In sidelong glances, hostile stares, and gruff behavior, I noticed the hostility among older kids and adults as well. We were all of Chinese descent, but we were still suspicious of each other. To have other Chinese kids cut their eyes at me or insult me in a language I couldn't understand embarrassed and humiliated me. And likewise, when I matched their chiding by disparaging them in English to my brothers, I'm sure I made them feel dumb.

Back then it had never occurred to me that my mother and grandmother had started out not speaking English, just like these girls I disdained. If my grandmother had been a young girl, and if we were meeting for the first time on this Chinese playground, we, too, would have been separated by language and customs. We might have been enemies simply because our rates of assimilation into American culture were staggered in time. But none of that mattered then. As a kid I was not making connections in my head about layers of experience within my cultural diaspora. I just wanted to hurl a ball at other kids' heads and laugh at them. Which is what my brothers and I did to them, and what they did to us.

Saturday was our day in Chinatown, but during the week my brothers and I also went to daily Chinese school after regular school. St. Mary's was the imposing gulag on the corner of Stockton and Clay Streets, and we reluctantly took the bus there from St. Brigid's on Franklin and Broadway Streets. Two schools and two sets of peers required switching personalities each afternoon. So from my efforts of being an American from 8:30 A.M. to 2:30 P.M., and then trying to be Chinese between 4:00 P.M. and 7:00 P.M., there was always a constant, consistent feeling of being not American enough, or not Chinese enough, or always lacking a little bit of both simultaneously.

To reconcile both sides of my life, I learned to remain safely vague and noncommittal when answering questions. I relied heavily on the time-tested phrase "I don't know" when talking to my peers. Girls from St. Brigid's asked, "Why don't you join Girl Scouts?" and instead of replying, "Because I have to go to Chinese school every afternoon," I just said, "I don't know." And at St. Mary's, when kids asked, "Why aren't you making kites and lanterns for Harvest Moon Festival?" once again I simply stated, "I don't know." It was a lot easier than explaining to ESL students that I had to glue together my Pilgrim diorama, memorize the Beatitudes, and finish a report titled "Gruesome Deaths of the Saints."

Back in those days, I was just making my way in my grammar-school-aged world. Although I started out as a little kid feeling totally comfortable in Chinatown, lovingly holding my grandma Lucy's hand as we strolled down the sidewalks, by the time I was a preteen, I already felt like a stranger in the community that first embraced my family.

Looking back now, I can't help but superimpose knowledge I've gained over the years—the history of Chinese gold seekers, coolie railroad workers, house servants, and thousands of little girls sold, stolen, or given away—on every memory I have of San Francisco's Chinatown.

Everything converges in my mind—my grandparents' early days, my own childhood memories, and the Chinese history I have since learned. All the information and feelings churn inside me as I walk, present day, down those same narrow city streets. I take in the garish colors and silent stares, bright souvenirs and dirty alleys. Glancing around, filled with both humility and pride, I know I am not alone. This convergence of past and present, of old and new, of quietude and bravado, is a particular melancholy familiar to almost every Chinese American.

4

The Defiant Chinese Body

As a kid, the conflict of feeling both Chinese and American continued to bubble inside me, cooling down or heating up to a rolling boil depending on where I was or whom I was with. Meanwhile, on the outside, my appearance caused its own quiet tension between me and those who inhabited my immediate surroundings. Unlike most other Chinese girls, I was not a flat-chested willow with noodly arms or a long, thin neck. I was a chunky chibbles. What kind of Chinese kid was I? The overweight, American kind.

Chuy! Why was I so chubby? No one would hug me, but pinching my blubber was a family pastime. My stomach, thighs, face, and legs were all up for grabs. I was a kid who lived mostly in my head, but these pinches of my tender flesh reminded me that my body was not just my own, but also somewhat community property as far as my family was concerned. It was a terrorism of teasing that was often shrugged away as being benign, but kept me feeling bad about myself, mixed up with love. My relatives poked me and said it was all in fun. Moreover, it was somehow supposedly for my own good. *You don't want to be fat, do you? But then . . . What—why aren't you eating? EAT! You're lucky you have food. Do you know there are starving people in China?* It made my elders happy to see me eat. Didn't I want to make them happy? *Oh. Now look at you. You're getting husky. Do you want to embarrass me?*

As a child, my body was being quietly, constantly scrutinized by adults. Parents, grandparents, extended relatives, and complete strangers could and would make comments out loud, or silently critique my physique with their smirks or expressions of disapproval. I learned to cover up, or run away.

Much has already been written about the impossible body standards that girls must navigate, but I think there is an added dimension in Asian culture. There is so much emphasis on saving face and reflecting well on your family that one is constantly scrutinized for the appearance of success. In the old days, maybe if you looked well fed, that could be considered an asset to your family, showing the community that your clan was wealthy and prosperous. That desire to parade you around like a prized pig is still there, and as always, your embarrassment or feelings are not valued. Your body is just one more way in which you reflect well or poorly on your parents and elders.

At times it seems that every Asian mom is genetically programmed to act like Waverly Jong's mother in *The Joy Luck Club.* Remember the scene in the movie when Tsai Chin struts down the street proudly displaying the magazine that shows

Waverly's chess championship photo? Every Asian mom wants your accomplishments, and hence her own, plastered on the front page so she can walk around triumphantly gloating.

And if you're a fatty, Mom can't gloat. Strangely, it is all about the gloating, isn't it? Or alternately, about saving face. And moms are never too pleased when your blubber is making your face unrecognizable, your skin swelling like a stretched-tight balloon that threatens to obscure your facial features. In my Wonder Woman T-shirt, I looked like a loaf of Wonder Bread, with eyes. People kept admonishing me to lose weight, but also kept feeding me. Then I was blamed for being Gigantor, like I was being embarrassing on purpose.

I was a fat kid. Maybe I couldn't express my dissatisfaction and melancholy in words, so I used my own body as a silent protest against perfection. Or maybe I packed on the pounds to protect myself from those who disapproved of me, to create a physical distance between me and them. Either way, being a jumbo prawn was just one way of being defiant.

For example, one time when I was little, my mom was trying to get me to do something, like vacuum, but I refused. We went back and forth in a typical way.

"Go do it."

"Why should I?"

"Because."

"Because why?"

"Because I said so."

"Why should I have to do whatever you say?"

My mom was so *over* my backtalk. She finally yelled, "Because I'm the person who MADE you!"

Oh, please. Was she really going there? I calmly retorted, "I came *through* you, but I am not *of* you."

That week at school we must have been studying prepositions and something about Jesus informing Joseph that he was but his earthly father.

My mom looked at me like I was nuts. Who was this little creep she had made? She stared at me mutely but was probably thinking she should start supervising my reading material.

After all these years, I still remember that exchange because it was such a clear moment in which I was declaring my separation from my mother. I didn't know it at the time, but from that moment onward, we were indeed on completely different wavelengths. She saw me as an extension of her own body and still wanted me to be an obedient baby. I was about ten years old and already considered myself an individual.

Another defining moment of separation between us came soon thereafter. One evening, after I had just brushed my teeth, I called to my mom to say that I was ready for bed. I waited in the hallway while she finished up whatever she was doing. I was hoping to win her attention and approval by making her laugh. As she approached, I stuck out my behind and pursed my lips in an exaggerated way like I'd seen on wooden, Chinese bobblehead dolls in a souvenir shop in Chinatown. I posed, bent at the waist and elbows akimbo with my lips out, ready for a smooch.

However, my attempt to delight her didn't go the way I planned. My mom recoiled from me and said, "If you're going to be disgusting, I'm not going to kiss you!"

Then she stormed off. And she never kissed me good night ever again.

I went to bed feeling like I'd done something wrong. As an adult now, thinking back, I wonder if my mom thought I was mocking her, or just being sassy, which wouldn't be tolerated.

Maybe she was worried about bills, or that I was displaying some kind of early, repugnant sexuality. Whatever the reason, the thing I remembered clearly was the operative word, *disgusting*.

Disgusting. That one moment in time, more than thirty years ago . . . how can I hold my mother responsible for one word, one moment in her own harried life as a person, wife, mother, daughter, secretary, and everything else she was and was trying to be for herself and others?

Disgusting. How could she possibly know that this one word would detonate a small but highly effective bomb throughout my psyche, body, and entire being? I have no way of knowing what was going on in my mother's head or heart back then. She was younger at the time than I am now.

But still. A word like that can sink into the pit of one's stomach like emotional shrapnel. As the years went on, I could form my flesh around that word, take that hard speck of grit, internalize it, and somehow make it into a pearl.

Or not. If my mom had bile crystallizing in her innards, it didn't have anything to do with me. As a matter of fact, years later my mother did have several gallstones removed. I remember when she returned home from the hospital, the doctor had given her the actual gallstones that had been taken out of her body. They were in a little plastic container and looked like tiny bits of black rock. Could they have been a physical manifestation of whatever was eating her up from the inside?

And most important, how can I take the formative experience of having been a pudgy kid, and the memory of my own mother calling me "disgusting," and do something positive? What might be the silver lining, if any? The resulting pearl is the fact that I have vowed to never make my own daughter feel anything even vaguely akin to disgusting to me. There are many physically repulsive aspects of life in a body, even a nine-year-old body, such as stomach flu, snot, grime, and everything else dirty, squishy, and smelly.

But my daughter is not disgusting. She is never disgusting. I teach her to take care of bodily functions. I am very aware of never belittling her or her body, the things she does, or what she is curious about. I respect her body and her privacy. And yes, I still kiss her good night.

5

Tough Love, Tough Luck

My parents constantly tell me I've got to "toughen up." But I'm a marshmallow, and I want to stay that way. They say I need to grow a backbone, but they're so stiff they can't even move.

We need to be soft and malleable inside because we have to be contortionists to work around our parents' fixed, hardened state. We might make them uncomfortable with our uncertainty, our tears, and our occasional moping. Maybe they believe that showing even a tiny bit of sympathy, or even acknowledging hardship or a tender heart, will cause a psychological upheaval so cataclysmic that all hell will break loose. Don't open Pandora's box, right?

But I don't want to be a sealed box. No air can even get in. I see a lot of these stiff, tight-lipped Chinese adults at family banquets, and they are so stoic and far away they might as well be in China. They are that inaccessible.

Parents, we adult children are messy, but we are what you've got. How about a compromise? How about controlled chaos, like nature in a sprawling state park, where there are some paths and paved trails, but flowers and foliage are still able to flourish? You're missing out on a potentially fantastic rose garden.

In the Sunset District of San Francisco where I once lived, there used to be a lot more small patches of grass and plants lining the walkways. Most homes were planned and built with two or more little plots of greenery, but as Chinese families moved into the houses, they ripped out the sod and any flowers, removed the dirt, and poured concrete over the area. Often they went one step further and painted the concrete green, as if this easy-to-clean slab of pavement was just as good as actual grass, but now improved with no mess and no fuss. My grandma Ruby once suggested we perform this same makeover on our entryway and balked when we declined to do so.

We liked it a little messy, with room to grow stuff. But she thought we were nuts. "Pave it, Kimi. So easy!"

More than anything, she was probably just miffed that we didn't follow her advice. But this is exactly what I'm talking about. I want to break through the Chinese concrete. It's a hardened mixture of filial piety, birth order, and saving face.

Even as I know I stand on the shoulders of many Chinese who came before me and suffered, I want the feeling of not being beholden 24 hours a day, 7 days a week, 365 days a year to someone else's standards and comparisons, susceptible to their praise and disappointment.

I want to be seen as myself.

And what is that self?

I, Marshmallow. I want to embrace vulnerability as a strength, not a weakness. If you're steel, or a watertight box, what's not getting in? Your baby's love. Her whispered secrets.

One night, when Lucy was almost asleep, she tugged me on the sleeve and quietly asked, "Mommy, are narwhals up at night?"

I was taken aback by her question. I hadn't known that she knew what narwhals were, nor did I even realize she was still awake. I was glad I had lingered at her bedside and had not immediately jumped up and run off to finish the dishes or brush my teeth. If I had been in too much of a rush I would have missed her sleepy, faraway imaginings of undersea life.

"Yes," I replied. "At least some of them are awake at night."

Our children are awake more than we know. And not just at night, but in life. Lucy's wakefulness opens my eyes to my relationship with my own parents. Since she is paying such close attention to everything I do, I am constantly reexamining my interactions with my own mom and dad, and it ain't always pretty.

I am a grown woman with a child of my own, but every time I return home from visiting my parents, I feel like I've gnawed off my own paw to escape the metal teeth of a spring-loaded trap. I scrape away at my own flesh and walk with a spiritual limp for a few days. I don't mean to hurt anyone by saying that. It is simply true. After spending too much time with my parents, it's like I have temporarily forgotten who I am, like I've received a blow to the head with a blunt instrument that is my family. Many adults are reduced to a regressed self in the company of their parents, but how many emotional body slams can we take before ending up with permanent *dain bramage*?

One physical reason for the headaches that develop during my visits is that there is always a lot of noise at my parents' house. A childhood friend of mine loves to imitate the way my mom used to say my name. My mother called me "Kimi," but it came out more like "Kimmaaaaaaay!"

My friend would jump out of her skin whenever she would hear it. I was accustomed to my mom's yelling, but even so, it did rattle my nerves. My mom, to this day, still continues to talk really loudly. Maybe it's because she grew up in a household with so many kids that you had to shout in order to be heard at all. Nonetheless, the tone and volume of her voice do add a drill sergeant quality to our relationship.

I remember once in high school, my mom was telling me something mundane, but she was hollering at such excessive volume that my hair was practically blowing in the breeze created by the force of her breath. I was right in front of her, but she might as well have been shouting across a stadium.

I couldn't take it anymore and said, "Stop screaming at me!"

She bellowed back, "This is my natural speaking voice!"

Adding further to the noise of the household, even if the volume of my mom's voice doesn't get to me: the constant squabbling and bickering among my family members, which wear me down to a nub, then continue to keep me on edge for hours afterward. I have an aunt who is constantly bragging to my mom about my cousins' careers. My mom once fought back by asking if my aunt's eldest daughter, who was then about fifty, had a boyfriend yet.

"*No, not yet . . .*" my aunt replied in a sweet yet seething sing-songy voice.

Later, in the car, I complained to my husband about how my mom and her siblings are constantly trying to one-up one another, and that my parents are always nitpicking everything, such as my choice of gas station where the price is two cents more per gallon than the gas at the station they prefer ten blocks away, or how I spread too much mayonnaise on a piece of bread, or how I pour too little water in the rice cooker. Nothing is safe without a comment here or a better way of doing things there, or a battle for the remote control, phone, or computer.

"Geez," I said as we drove away from their house. "In addition to all that shouting, do they have to have every ringer, television, and radio on all at the same time, and every single one on the highest volume possible?"

My husband, Rolf, countered, "Don't you think it's about time you eased up on your mom?"

"No, not yet . . ."

In my head I can already hear people saying that this micromanaging is how parents show they love you. They'd say to me, "You are lucky someone cares enough about you to tell you these things."

I know, I know, I know. But tell that to the bloody stump where my hand used to be.

In Chinese families, the undertow of guilt and filial piety is as strong as the riptide at Ocean Beach. But do you know what the posted signs say on the seawall? PEOPLE WADING AND SWIMMING HAVE DROWNED HERE.

Nonetheless, I do have sympathy and compassion for my mom. I know she had to work very hard from a very young age. I do understand that. She worked in souvenir shops in Chinatown, and also in doctors' offices after school as a teenager up until early adulthood. Her younger siblings took up my grandma's time, and Mom and her older sister had to work while they watched their sisters and brother grow up with more than they ever got.

My mom and her sister Jeannette were tough immigrant kids. They were tossed into public school knowing not a word of English. Other kids called them fresh-off-the-boat, and they were. They had no toys, helped their mom and dad, and raised all the younger kids to boot. As my grandparents became more prosperous, eventually having their own travel agency in Chinatown, my mom and Jeannette watched their siblings become self-indulgent American beatniks, hippies, and, later, disco aficionados. Chinese translation: lazybones, deadbeats, good-for-nothings.

It is not for naught that my mom, whose name is Irene, is known in some circles as I Ream. Or for short, just the Reamer.

Growing up, I frequently heard my mother yelling at her siblings, saying things like, "Get up, and get a job," or "You are going to end up just another no-good bum," or "You act so stupid, it's sickening!"

One can see that before she was a Tiger Mom, my mom was already a Tiger Sister. She had plenty of experience disdaining her siblings, so by the time her own children came along, she had her reaming ways down pat.

Which came in mighty handy for her as she dealt with my brothers and me. As we grew older, my mom spent every weekday morning, for years, making breakfast and our sack lunches, and she drove us to three different schools on opposite ends of town. Then she headed off to work as an executive secretary for demanding doctors. From 9:00 A.M. to 5:00 P.M. she was expected to make the nurses' schedules, distribute payroll, comfort families, and fetch lunch. Then she'd pick us up from her mother's place, drive us back across the city, and come home to a house that we had destroyed the night before with our rear-ranging of couch cushions into play forts. I'm sure she loved being confronted nightly with the disheveled, chaotic results of our many hours of Nerf basketball, Nerf football, and Nerf . . . war. Then she would have to make dinner and somewhere in there say hello to my dad who'd get home at eight o'clock.

Thank goodness my mom was a Jedi master at all things practical, and here I am complaining that I didn't get enough hugs?

Pretty much.

To be tough is what Chinese parents want their kids to be. When I was little, I would try to hug my parents and they would wonder what the heck I was trying to do. "Uh, okay, enough, enough," they would say, patting me awkwardly on the back, or on the forearm. I was always writing little love notes and slip-ping them into my mom's purse or under my parents' pillows, but they just sort of *endured* it. I was otherwise quiet enough, so they let my weirdness slide.

Many different parents of various ethnicities believe the world is a tough place, so they've got to make their babies tough. Chinese parents have somehow taken this idea and merged it with a competitive drive. When she wasn't reaming us out for our messiness and bad behavior, my mom consistently bragged about her friends' children. She most likely was trying to spur me on. But instead, I just felt *spurned* by her, never being good enough to please her.

She would say things like, "Have you heard about Caitlin? She's going to Stanford," or "Janet had a beautiful wedding at the Olympic Club." My mom excelled at making me feel like crap for my own supposed benefit.

Once she said, "Did you see that So-and-So's daughter teaches aerobics? She has such a great body. Isn't it great that she's so slender?"

Of course, then I had to lash out.

"Yeah. Too bad she's a butterface. Everything looks good. But her face."

"You're just mean."

"That's right. You have a fat, mean daughter. Your friends' daughters are skinny and sweet. Too bad they're all butterfaces."

"I don't know how you got this way."

"You don't? I thought you *made* me."

Ka-ching! My mom kind of recoiled from that one. I guess she needed to toughen up.

I still kinda feel bad about that exchange. So much so that I still remember saying those words, three decades later. Obviously, when someone consistently makes you feel rotten, sometimes ya just snap and give in to the temptation to fight fire with fire. But when I think about the kind of person I really want to be, I wouldn't ever want my mother to feel like she had to toughen up because of me, or away from me, or in order to protect herself from any armor I developed to combat her.

That's how the dark side sucks you in. Even if you don't want to, you may find yourself still moving toward it. As a kid I was already caught in the tractor beam, and it was pulling me in.

6

Origin of the Tiger Mother Species

Tiger Mothers. Okay, what exactly are we talking about here? We're talking no hugs, no sweet nothings whispered into your soft little ears, not even a smooch good night. Tiger Moms aren't exactly cuddly cupcakes. They don't kiss your boo-boos when you stumble and scrape the skin off your leg. Tiger Moms are, shall we say, detached. Practical to a fault. I was fed and clothed just fine, and I know I should be thankful for that. But what of the abstract, less concrete gestures, those that we most define as "mothering"? Where is that, Tiger Lady? What about nurturing, reassuring, and . . . loving?

Sorry. It's illegal to import that. You'll never get it through customs.

My own mother has always been blunt and matter-of-fact. There were never any romantic Mary Cassatt moments between

us. Of course, Mary Cassatt had no kids. All those sweet paintings of mother and child were all wishful thinking. Who else
had no kids? Beatrix Potter, the artist whose creations charmed
a century of mothers and babies. Maybe they had the ability to
conjure those nurturing, feminine ideals because no one was
yelling, "Mommy, Mommy, Mommy," in their faces while demanding mac 'n' cheese, *Ruby Gloom* cartoons, and rapt attention to the plight of their Transformers.

I try to understand where this Tiger Mom vibe came from
in the first place. First off, I remember that life might be comfortable for Tiger Moms now, but their hard-assery comes from
having been poor as children. Also, they themselves were dis-
criminated against and, most likely, more openly and harshly
than we are now.

Tiger Parents have developed this practical approach from
a young age because they had to. Chinese families were often
big and rowdy, and their own parents probably ruled with absolute authority and corporal punishment. When our parents
were kids, they didn't have time to get all weepy because they
probably had to help in the family business whether it was food
service, laundry, sewing piecework, or whatever else under the
sun Chinese families did to survive. Also, there was the raising of younger siblings, and everyone lived crammed together
without any semblance of privacy. Therefore, to them, our feelings of being inconvenienced by the smallest infraction of our
personal space must be pretty laughable. When their parents
knocked them in the head with a raised third knuckle or pulled
their ears, they swallowed their pride, turned the other cheek,
and learned how to get tough.

I often wonder what my life would have been like as a Chinese American woman if I'd been born in other eras. From

1860 to 1900, I would have been lucky to be the daughter of a shopkeeper or the wife of a merchant. My days would have passed mostly indoors, as Chinese women hardly left the house for reasons of safety or Confucian ideology, which promoted bound feet as a measure to ensure a lack of independence. I would have raised the children and tended to the food, and possibly would have helped roll cigars, bait fish hooks, or do other menial tasks. But more than likely, if I were a Chinese woman during that time in California, I would have been a prostitute, having been kidnapped, sold by my own family, or even auctioned off several times to lead a dismal life.

In those days I also could have been a laundryman's daughter and I might've been glad to be sequestered in steamy squalor, soaking dirt-caked clothes in boiling water and lifting a ten-pound iron to smooth over the clean clothes. I would have had burn marks all over my hands from the strenuous work, but at least I wouldn't have had to suffer gazes from white barbarians out on the street.

Meanwhile, Chinese men were exploited for cheap labor in railroad construction, agriculture, and a variety of service jobs deemed too menial by white workers. The newspapers and magazines of the era frequently caricatured the Chinese as rats, both for the perception of dirtiness and of swarming plenitude. Movies and popular stories of that time frequently depicted Chinatowns as places for murder, kidnapping, and the corruption of whites by sexually depraved inhabitants who stupefied their victims with opium.

However, in San Francisco the climate did slowly and painstakingly begin to change for Chinese Americans. After the 1906 earthquake, the new, rebuilt Chinatown was sanitized and made pretty for tourists with ornate balconies and bright streetlamps.

It was hailed as an area ready for more Americanization and commerce, with less vice and corruption. Back in China, the Qing Dynasty collapsed, and a new stage for upheaval was set. Sun Yat-sen founded the Republic of China in 1912, but by 1915 political chaos reigned with conflicting warlords vying for power. Sun died in 1925, and by 1927, his successor, Chiang Kai-shek and his Nationalist party, the Kuomintang, did not fare better in unifying China. The Nationalists and the opposing Communists inadvertently killed thousands of civilians as they vied for control of the country.

Meanwhile, in the United States, Chinese American women living from the 1920s to 1940s may have been cautious but longed to be carefree, were strong but perceived as weak, might have been adventurous yet stayed back because of family loyalty or lack of opportunity. They joined the ranks of thousands of restaurant workers, house servants, elevator girls, and sewing women. They worked in many nonglamorous but necessary moneymaking endeavors, in any jobs that were available to them. Some married and moved to rural areas, while others remained humble Chinatown residents, some of whom I viewed as a child after they had grown old. These young women of the 1920s and 1930s became the old ladies of the early 1970s who pulled their grim expressions of hardship into sad smiles while they watched me toddle across the street. If I was with my grandma Lucy, they were the ones who stopped to chat, and exclaimed how lucky I was, while I obliviously and petulantly pulled my grandmother toward the Baskin-Robbins ice cream shop on Grant Avenue.

If I were a grown Chinese American woman in the 1920s and 1930s, maybe I would have been one of the ladies I've seen in pictures of the Chinatown Telephone Exchange. I may have had an American hairstyle with pin curls or finger waves, but might have still worn a traditional Chinese dress. Few Chinese women would have donned the outfit of a flapper, as did Anna May Wong who danced the Charleston in 1922 for *East Is West*. Most likely, one's clothing would be modest, because even in the 1940s a Chinese person could still be refused a clerical job at a business simply because of her race. Companies would simply state, "We don't hire Chinese."

A Chinese American woman back then would no doubt have been keenly aware of Madame Chiang Kai-shek, who toured America in 1943 to raise support for China. She was elegant and spoke perfect English and was a symbol of a new China—pro-American, Christian, and, style-wise, a complete knockout.

Who was this woman? In 1937, *Life* magazine called Madame Chiang Kai-shek "probably the most powerful woman in the world." She was the wife of the president of China, and she single-handedly charmed the world leaders of the West into believing, for a brief time anyway, that China wanted democracy and modernity. And how did she do it? By speaking English fluently with a disarming southern lilt, and with legs down to there and a cheongsam slit up to here.

Interestingly, while she worked the visual allure of her sexuality to the utmost advantage, in words she sought to downplay her "otherness."

Madame Chiang Kai-shek is famously known for saying, "The only Chinese thing about me is my face."

Ah so. A new kind of butterface.

She was a twentieth-century fox, and she knew how to use her body, her demeanor, and the power of her beauty. Chinese people who remember that era think of her with pride as someone who was accepted on the international stage as an equal in a time of vast inequalities and racism. Without her, China in the 1930s and 1940s would have had no equivalent of a good-will ambassador who embodied hope and elegance. Madame Chiang Kai-shek rose to prominence by simultaneously playing up her exoticism and denying she was Chinese at all. WTF! Apparently, though, she gave the world what it wanted to see and hear.

With China joining the Allied Powers after the Japanese attack on Pearl Harbor, Chinese American women could now participate in war relief work. They raised funds, worked in defense plants, and even served in the armed forces. World War II gave both male and female Chinese Americans the opportunity to become more integrated into American society as a whole. Now Chinese American women were able to get jobs in businesses that were previously unavailable because of race. Careers were now an option in private industries, just as they now were for American women as a whole. Opportunities in more sectors of professional life became increasingly available.

By the 1950s, prosperity had come to many Chinese American families, including my own. In photos of my relatives' high school classes, the Chinese gals wear cat-eye glasses, pedal pushers, and teenybopper outfits identical to those of their blond-haired, blue-eyed classmates. In other pictures from this decade, I've come across Chinese American girls in bathing suit contests, or dressed as cheerleaders, or sitting in soda fountains, all resembling black-haired Bettys and Veronicas from *Archie* comics.

As far as the 1960s are concerned, I don't picture too many young, Chinese American women running off to become flower children, despite Chinatown's relative proximity to Golden Gate Park. During this decade, Chinese Americans were still working diligently to achieve their goals of assimilation. Despite the phenomenon of San Francisco's Haight-Ashbury scene at the time, I think there was a huge disconnect between America's then-burgeoning counterculture and Chinese Americans. We weren't ready yet to embrace hippie insouciance and bad hygiene. In contrast, many were still holding on to their identity as patriotic Americans. Those second-generation Number One Sons had just earned their engineering degrees on the GI Bill and went to work for Boeing and Lockheed Corporation. We were still pursuing the American Dream, not trying to debunk its myths and dismantle it.

In the 1970s, I was just a kid in a *Star Wars* T-shirt, riding my banana-seat bicycle and making detailed drawings of R2-D2 and C-3PO after Chinese school and piano lessons. I was eating rice gruel with salted pork and washing that fatty Chinese goodness down with a Shamrock Shake.

At that time, my mother's youngest siblings boasted feathered hair, KC and the Sunshine Band records, and Camaros. I watched them with fascination as they talked about dates, making out, and drinking tequila sunrises at local fern bars like Henry Africa's and Lord Jim's. Would I have been like them if I had been an adult then? I'd like to think not, but who knows?

As it was, in the 1980s I morphed into a Flock of Seagulls fan with a wedge hairdo. It was during this period that *Newsweek* put Asian Americans on its cover, declaring us model minorities. Ice skater Tiffany Chin was the latest incarnation of the Asian good girl, Connie Chung was on TV, and the model Ariane starred with Mickey Rourke in *Year of the Dragon*. Movies like *Big Trouble in Little China* and *Tai-Pan* were evidence that Hollywood still projected Asians through a distorted lens, but I did see enough Asian representation in the media to feel like any profession was within my grasp. There were local newscasters like Jan Yanehiro on *Evening Magazine,* and bylines by Ben Fong-Torres in *Rolling Stone.* I didn't particularly feel like a minority, especially in San Francisco.

And I guess I wasn't. At the time, criticism was just coming to the forefront regarding the University of California and admissions requirements that were possibly biased against Asian Americans. Apparently, we were outperforming white applicants on either test scores or GPAs or both and were being held to higher standards in order to be offered acceptance letters. The bottom line was that the order of the universe might have come crashing down if there were more Asians than whites on campus. Well, so much for thinking we were ideal minorities. Now we were just too good for our own good, and our numbers needed to be controlled. It was 1987, but hadn't we heard "The Chinese Must Go" one hundred years earlier? Admissions requirements were subsequently tweaked and retweaked, and to this day the debates rage on about affirmative action and racial quotas in college admissions.

The options for Chinese women in America have evolved from limited to limitless. The doors of access have been thrown open so we can now achieve the pinnacle of every field. So naturally, it seems, Chinese women would crush any and all competition on the playing field of motherhood, too, right?

But raising and loving human beings is different from studying for tests and rising through the professional ranks. In academics and the corporate world, crucial skills that lead to success are memorization, the application of logic, and delineating sharp goals and adhering to those lines and properties. Parenthood, however, is not about memorization but requires total improvisation. You must deal with your gurgling spawn whose non-sequitur style of talking and bathroom needs defy logic. And last, in this new reality, all concepts of hygiene, discipline, social hierarchy, and sometimes morals become blurred. Boundaries once clearly drawn, as well as your sanity, dissolve.

Motherhood is not about outlining a foolproof plan, because none exists when it comes to your baby. So when all your skills of diligence and exactitude prove to be ineffective, how can you not just succeed, but win? Failure is most certainly never an option. So maybe women who are accustomed to high levels of perfection then take the logical route, and just try to clamp down harder to gain control of an uncontrollable situation.

Et voilà! That's when the Tiger Mother enters stage right. (And of course, she is always right.)

The Tiger Mom is like a modern, virulent strain of the dragon lady that, with each generation, becomes more and more resistant to the human body's natural ability to fight back. And we are the ones who've let this infectious personality rage out of control and ravage our systems. Tiger Babies, there are currently no antibiotics that can help us combat this formidable foe that flows through our bloodstreams. Our hearts will have to pump out the courage to fight back with love and empathy for our Tiger Parents. They are missing the chromosome for tenderness, and we must somehow be the stem cell donors to help them.

The generations that came before us were working so hard to survive, to earn money, and to get a foothold in work and society that many of us were left to raise ourselves. Or at least that's what it felt like. Even if we were lucky enough to have food and clothes, and our other basic needs were otherwise provided for, we did not necessarily ever feel emotionally, psychologically, or spiritually sustained.

Chinese Americans have achieved so much from the first waves of immigration to the present. The next frontier is an abstract one. We are not strangers on a different physical shore, but in our hearts and minds. Our houses may be already built, but we the children of the first and second generations are still begging to be let in.

Let me in, Mom. I know the door to your heart isn't rusted shut.

7

Rise of the 3.2 GPAs

There ought to be an explanatory parable:

The Maker of the Universe gave Chinese people many attributes: ambition, perseverance, and nearsightedness. But the day when emotional availability was being handed out, Chinese people were too busy shopping at Costco, and forcing their kids to play piano. Plus, this emotional availability thing seemed to be not very expensive, and of very poor quality. So they disregarded it. Blew it off. It didn't seem like anything they needed, especially because it didn't seem to impress their friends, make money, taste good, or denote status. They sniffed at it and said, "Eh."

But when their kids and grandkids moved to America, achieved great successes, but then refused to come visit, the Chinese people got a vague whiff that maybe that emotional availability thing might have had some use after all. But they couldn't admit they had made a mistake. So instead they just called their children lazy and blamed them for liking non-Chinese things such as cheddar cheese.

Over time, the parents began to buy five-pound hunks of Tillamook at Costco, but sentimentality is still, even to this day, unavailable in bulk at discount stores.

Now that Chinese Americans have indeed attained and achieved so much, can we be big enough to admit that we are not Number One all the time?

Through many generations of physical and mental perseverance, backbreaking work, and the swallowing of our pride, Chinese people have always held steadfast to the concept of The Best. We like to think that we are the best at doing everything. We raise the best kids. We own and consume the best name brands. Chinese people are THE BEST. I guess it's inevitable that when the best doesn't quite work out, we've also got the best rate of offing ourselves. So we're the best, even in death. Those stupid other races. They think they can compete with Chinese! We even have suicide dialed.

My aunt who said I'd be a loser without a Mercedes-Benz? Her sister killed herself by jumping off the Golden Gate Bridge before she turned twenty-seven years old. There's a connection somehow. That's proof right there that something sucks in Chinese thinking.

Wake up, overachievers. Wake up, underachievers. No one has to kill themselves anymore. We adhered to standards of superiority because throughout our history we have been treated blatantly as inferior. No wonder we subsequently claimed to have invented everything good: ice cream, spaghetti, pugs, the color pink, potstickers, and superior parenting à la Tiger Mom.

But now that we are sitting pretty, or at least have secured a growing claim to the American middle class, could we now ease up on the posture that we are the best at everything?

Not every Chinese kid is going to play Carnegie Hall, have his or her picture taken with the president of the United States, or become a city supervisor or state assemblywoman. We aren't all filet mignon. Statistically, some of us have to be the cheap cuts. Some of us are just stew meat.

The emperor of China has no clothes, but no one is talking about anything. And somebody has got to say something. Asian people usually won't voluntarily expose their own shortcomings, pain, petty jealousies, or embarrassing moments. That leaves a writer with only herself as subject matter. I hope that sharing my utterly human, world-class, stupid mistakes might drill a tiny hole in the Great Wall of Chinese silence. For you, Kind Reader, I undertake this alarming task with my bare hands. My only tools are words that I've linked together like a chain of paper clips. I hope that what I've written can pull someone through.

Anyone.

People like you and me.

Because of the hardships they endured, or maybe because they still have one foot in the old world, our Tiger Moms and Tiger Dads might never stop pushing us toward being the best. They might never concede that without being absolutely number one we are still fine people, or good sons and daughters. If we are just fairly accomplished in our careers, have great kids of our own, or are happy individuals or kind human beings, our achievements are somehow never enough for our Tiger Parents.

Then to add insult to injury, as time goes by, our stoic, unyielding, older parents will only see the past through their rose-colored eyewear. "What are you complaining about?" they might say. They are good at pretending not to notice the faint scars—on our bodies, our psyches, and our hearts. They'll shrug off any beatings we endured, saying we succeeded because of their toughness, not despite it.

We adult children of Tiger Parents want acknowledgment of the deep pains, emotional or physical, that our moms and dads caused. We want an apology. We might settle for an admission of regret, but we might never even get that.

My brother once confronted our mother about the spankings he suffered as a child. He was very brave to even bring up the subject. But her response was not all that satisfying. Our mother said, "If that did happen to you, then I am sorry."

Please notice the evasive wording. I'm not sure how my mom can still sometimes mix up the pronouns *he* and *she,* but in a pinch, she instantaneously mastered the English language's conditional verb tense. Her sentence left plenty of room for interpretation. She did not at all own up to anything, really. And that totally sucked.

So in this way, when attempting to confront Tiger Parents, one might experience the futility in hauling them in for questioning. Our requests for accountability might never stick. They somehow always make bail.

They are not the ones in jail.

We are.

We are in emotional jail, on emotional death row.

Tiger Babies, since we can't do anything about our elders' emotional availability, maybe at least we can do something for ourselves.

Let's stop pretending that all this jockeying to be the best is working for any of us. Let's stop leasing those luxury cars for appearance's sake, and rise up in our hoopties to declare that we are here, so get used to us. Let's throw away those report cards, because we're not in high school anymore.

What matters is who we are now.

PART 2

Peek Behind the Curtain

8

A Tale of Two Runts

If Chinese families can have Tiger Moms, then inevitably there must be Tiger Runts, *n'est-ce pas*? No one will admit to their existence. They live, but they are shunted aside. Passed over. Insulted and hidden away. Just like in the wild, the weak are often left to perish. And yet here we are, not going away anytime soon.

We are oftentimes the youngest children in our families, we the artists, writers, truth tellers, and whistle-blowers. We are the deal breakers. This statement does not come from scientific evidence. I'm just saying that some of us are usually the ones who are accommodating everyone. We change our schedules to fit around parents and elder children because everyone else is more adept at playing My Time Is More Important Than Yours.

How many daughters are out there like me, just doing every-thing because . . . just because? We've always been marshmallows, but now we've been left out in the cold so long that we're starting to develop an unpleasant crust.

Unpleasant crust, here we come!

I think when a woman turns forty she has the right to finally decide she's no longer gonna do crap she doesn't wanna do. I'm busy and I'm tired.

When is enough, enough? For some, never. I have a few relatives who will live with their parents until the very end. They are not boomerang babies, going off to college and then returning to freeload for the rest of their lives. Rather, they never left. They are the family sacrifices. As hard as it is to say, there are some Asian parents who will willfully keep down a child just to ensure that they themselves will never be alone. It's a big thing in Chinese culture: Who will look after me when I'm old? Who will tend to my grave? Get over it, Granny! You've ruined your kid's life just so you wouldn't have to watch TV alone. Just so you could have someone to complain to, and to keep down.

I've seen it happen. And it happens a lot to youngests. What, exactly, is happening here? You are clung to and kept at home. You are the default maid, butler, companion, surrogate spouse, best friend, and adult child forever. You are kept alive to serve others. You might look just fine from the outside, but out in public, on your invisible choke chain called Love, you look shell-shocked. Your parents still monitor your every move and won't or can't let you go. As the father says to the son in *Flower Drum Song*, "When that day come when you can think for yourself, I will let you know!"

Except that your Chinese parents might never let you know. Maybe you're the most succulent piglet of the litter, and they believe no one will ever be good enough for you. Or, conversely, they can take the opposite tactic and make you think no one will love or tolerate you but them. Either way, they've pulled you in like the Death Star with magnetic power, and you can't escape.

Perhaps you are just collateral damage. A Tiger Parent who exalts one kid into high achievement might keep you on the side to quell his or her loneliness while Number One is off ruling the world. Hey, someone's gotta stay home and do the dishes. Someone's gotta dust the portraits of accomplished Chinese Americans like Michelle Kwan that your parents place prominently on top of the outdated VCR seemingly just to mock you.

It's all very unfair, and we have to not fall for these parental ruses. Maybe the parents themselves don't even know they are pushing us into these limited roles. Your brother is off to Little League, but you stay with your mom. Or your sister is off to dance class, but you stay at home. Are you the sacrifice? Maybe you are too shy to do anything, but by the time you decide you can risk making a peep to express your outside interests, it's too late. Maybe the family has become dependent on your staying home. You might not even be out of your teens, but your role in your family, and in life, has already swallowed you whole.

I have one family friend like this. I'll call her Allison. Strangely enough, her birth order blows my theory because she is, in fact, the eldest of her siblings. But this does happen, too. In her case, starting from childhood, she had always been The Favorite. As Allison got older, it was as if her mom really couldn't bear the thought of her dearest darling out in the world. Maybe the mom transferred all her own fears onto Allison, and to make sure nothing bad ever happened to her, she didn't let anything at all happen to her, not even the potentially good things. So Allison's mom shrank her world, until there was only mom to live for.

Allison is always by her mother's side. She doesn't go anywhere or do anything without her mother. She is a grown woman, now way past forty. She cooks and cleans, and what else does she do all day? She is in the house, sleeping in the twin bed where she slept as a child, the empty bunk beds of her siblings who've all left home still stacked there. The old beds are abandoned, still affixed with their decals and stickers, left there with only Allison for company. It's just Allison and the old stuffed animals, with her parents in the adjacent room.

Creepy. Safe. A catch-22.

She's taken care of financially. She will always have a roof over her head, and her clothing and food are provided. Her mom takes her shopping at department stores, and they go to the grocery store and she does have some say in what gets bought. But she doesn't drive. Never goes on dates, and never has. She will never be a hostess at her own party or have her own friends. In a way, she is just like a Victorian spinster, except with a flat-screen TV and a freezer full of salted caramel gelato.

She is in the locked Chinese box. But maybe she doesn't even know she is in one. Or maybe she has realized it and has decided to make the best of it. I don't know. I wonder if she ever tried the doorknob and found it locked, or maybe being locked in is the only way she can function at all. I doubt anyone ever asked her if she wanted to go to college, move anywhere, or have her own life away from the family. Perhaps she likes it that way.

Maybe Allison has found a certain freedom in never having to worry about working, having a significant other, or caring for a dependent child of her own. Technically, she can do whatever she likes with her time, provided it takes place inside her parents' house. Perhaps I am simply unable to see the upside of such an arrangement.

Allison's parents have let her other siblings go. They have lives, jobs, friends, and romantic relationships. But, hey, then again, who says Allison can't be happy? For all I know, she has a slamming inner life and is really into fan fiction and has an outrageous online persona known by millions as NakedUnderMyCape3000.

Every time I see an Asian American family with an adult kid like Allison on a tight tether, it strikes me as against type that any Chinese parent would keep any of their kids from a path of ambition. Nonetheless, I think it's pretty common. We just don't hear very much about it because these adult kids never leave the freaking house.

Rock on, NakedUnderMyCape3000!

Or . . . what am I saying? Don't rock on, NakedUnderMyCape3000! Bust outta there, for heaven's sake. Grab some chopsticks and dig a tunnel under the washing machine. Is it too late for you? It's never too late. Find a way to change yourself. Don't settle for not speaking up.

Maybe give someone a sign.

Give *me* a sign, at the next Family Association dinner. After all, we are both hiding in plain sight.

I might be sociable on the outside, but I feel like a separate person inside. It's the only way I know how to be. As I think about you, Allison, maybe we are more alike than I realize. We are similar animals in a shared landscape. I see you crouched there in the sagebrush. You see that I see you. I see you because I'm coiled behind the rock, at your same eye level. We spy on each other from this low vantage point.

But I don't think we're concealing ourselves for the same reasons. In fact, who's hiding and who's hunting is indiscernible. We're both as still as stones, calm as unrippled water. We both appear as if we have all day to wait here, but either one of us could bolt at any moment, if we have to.

Shy Allisons of the world, hiding in your Chinese American enclosures, I see you, and you see me. We are two fuzzy creatures, one behind the fence, another out in the meadow. The houses are just beyond, and I wonder if we have an unspoken pact; I won't let anyone know that I saw you, even if I get captured.

I'll watch where you get taken. Signal me if you can.

You've been crouched there in the sage for a very long time. I've been observing you. You've got one eye slightly larger than the other. When you are weary, I've noticed that your right eye gets squinty.

I know you're thinking what I'm thinking. Even if no one knows, even if no one recognizes it, I can see that you have very serious aspirations. Even if you are the only player, the game is still on.

You feel the blood gurgling in your throat. No matter how captivated the world is with entertainment's distractions, for you the internal world still remains. Just as it remains and waits for me as well. We tune in to it. We can still hear ourselves think, even if we don't share our thoughts with anyone. People drink alcoholic beverages to drown out their inner voices, the humming and birdsong. Can you still discern the deep growling, and five-year-olds' laughter? Some children's eyes have only seen innocence, and a part of that remains in you.

But you are afraid of breaking out of your routine. You know there's danger in the shallows. You can still drown in two inches of bathwater.

If you won't give someone a sign of your desire to change, no one can help you. Allison, give me a sign. I'll be waiting.

* * *

Likewise, on my dad's side of the family, Uncle Bill was a Tiger Runt, for sure. My grandma Ruby was the eldest of seven children, and he was the last born of her siblings, and the most timid. If the meek really do inherit the earth, Uncle Bill must own prime real estate on all seven continents. He would've made Walter Mitty look like a rock star.

Uncle Bill had wanted to marry a girl named Christine. I am not sure if she had Down syndrome or any other specific ailment, but the general consensus from what older relatives will actually tell me is that she was not in perfect, A-plus, gonna-play-at-Carnegie-Hall condition. But Bill and Christine were inseparable. They even went to the same Health Farm for Misfit Broken Toys in Santa Rosa in the 1940s because they were both asthmatics.

After Uncle Bill died, I found a lovingly cared-for photo album with pictures of the two of them chastely feeding pigeons and enjoying each other's company. I asked my aunts what had happened to them. Apparently, my grandmother Ruby busted them up. She was Bill's older sister, and since their parents were deceased, I suppose she had de facto Tiger Mom jurisdiction over him and effectively got rid of Christine. Grandma Ruby didn't throw her down a well or anything, but I imagine she somehow told Christine's family to keep her retarded ass away from her little brother.

When I remarked to my mother that what happened with Bill and Christine was really horrible, in a moment of surprising clarity, my mom shrugged and rhetorically asked, "See what happens when you listen to your family?"

As I knew him, Uncle Bill was a very downtrodden man. As far as I could tell, one of his small pleasures in life was to collect decorative hors d'oeuvres toothpicks embossed with the names of the touristy places he visited—Niagara Falls, Honolulu, Las Vegas—but when he died, the packaged souvenirs were all thrown out unused, having never been opened.

Maybe you could say Bill himself was unused and unopened. He was very shy, and he suffered when Christine had been deemed not good enough. A dud. The Chinese ladies had clucked their tongues, and that was that.

So Bill did not marry Christine.

In addition to photos of the "health camp," in the album there were pictures of Uncle Bill at the U.S. Postal Service office where he worked, sorting big metal baskets of mail. Also, there was a snapshot of him in front of a plaque that read WELCOME TO WAIKIKI! In the background was a swaying palm tree, and the sky was light blue and peaceful. Bill was wearing a button-down, long-sleeved shirt, a wide black tie, a sweater vest, wool slacks, and black leather shoes, and he had a raincoat folded in his arms.

I wanted to say, "Hey, Uncle Bill, good thing ya got that raincoat. You never know when a hailstorm might strike."

And how, you might wonder, did I come across this sad little photo album and the unused cocktail toothpicks?

Because I'm the one who threw out the detritus of his entire life. When his siblings decided it was time to move him to assisted living, my husband and I cleaned out his house. We scrubbed the urine off the floors and walls and sorted and recycled junk mail, bills, holiday cards, and vital records going back to 1952. We chiseled off decayed food from the kitchen tile and arranged for Sunset Scavenger to take away sixty-four Hefty bags full of his belongings.

There were grade-school report cards, long-expired prescription bottles, tax records from two decades ago, and a junk pile full of personal items. But this stuff hadn't been junk to him. It was his life. I tried to call around to family members to ask if they wanted to save his things, but for every person I phoned, each said the exact same thing: throw that crap out.

No one could deal with it. No one wanted old photos, cheap dishes, documents, *Living with Houseplants,* mini weenie forks, souvenir toothpicks, or any gadget ordered from late-night television ads: the coin-flushing bank, lamps that strapped onto your forehead, fake leather satchels, or Chia Pets. Throw it out. Get rid of it. Salvation Army. How the heck should I know? Why are you calling *me*? Who *is* this?

It's Kim. I'm your niece. *You* know, Larry and Irene's kid. Yeah, Number Three.

Yes, I was reduced to my birth-order number. Fine. Once they'd ascertained who the hell I was, the answer was still the same: throw that crap out.

I wanted to know more about Bill's life, but I didn't get much out of anybody. No one knew anything, or else they just said nothing. Nothing and everything was none of my freaking business so don't ask; just stuff your face with long-life noodles at the next Chinese banquet and shut the hell up, Number Three.

Well, okay then.

Uncle Bill was a Tiger Baby. A non–Carnegie Hall player. A runt. He was one of us and was stomped down by life. He lived as an invisible Chinese man. His big sis, my grandma Ruby, put the hammer down and he pretty much didn't put up a fight. She was fierce, all right. But at what cost?

As a kid, I would see my grandmother berating Uncle Bill at family dinners. He sat like a lump and took it. Chinese people have used passivity as a survival strategy for centuries, but sometimes I really wish he had stood up to her, even once. But I guess he just didn't have it in him to fight.

I think of Uncle Bill often. And as I write this I wonder, am I telling his secrets or am I keeping his spirit a little bit alive? At his funeral I couldn't bear to speak about the little, poignant things I learned about him while throwing out his life's nibbles and bits. It was freezing in Colma that day, and the few of us who were there stood in a tiny huddle. I was blubbering cuz that's what I do. My grandmother, who'd lain down the law and deemed the LUV of his life a loser, didn't even get out of the car. Of course, she was in her nineties and it was ass-cold, so I'll cut her some slack, but dang.

They lowered Bill's smallish casket into the Astroturf-lined pit and I wished, suddenly, that I had placed some of his beloved souvenir toothpicks in there with him. Maybe he could have the cocktail party in heaven that he couldn't, or simply didn't, have here.

He was never Number One. I never saw him in any holiday photo. No one would have ever called him the best or brightest of anything. He was a dim star in a packed Milky Way of high-achieving, Chinese superstars. But let me stop and say that Uncle Bill mattered. He came and went quietly without a peep, but he was just like so many of us. He may never have achieved any conventional hallmarks of greatness, and wasn't particularly good-looking, didn't excel in his profession, have children, or even drive a cool car. In fact, he didn't even have a license. But it didn't mean he didn't have wants and needs, or dreams as big as anyone else's. Who was he? He was a Tiger Cub who never spoke up, struck back, or even talked back. There are thousands of us, millions even, all alone inside ourselves.

And to further remind myself that gentle souls always matter, I keep Bill's picture on the refrigerator. No one ever asks me about it. No one has asked me who he is. And I have not pointed him out to anybody. But he is there. And I know it. Oftentimes, at potluck dinners with our neighbors, I find myself talking to someone in my kitchen but I'm looking slightly to the side, to the picture of him. My friends and I might be laughing and having a good time. We have appetizers and drinks, but we've got no cocktail toothpicks from the Grand Canyon. I stand there remembering Bill as my friend talks. Despite the fact that I barely knew him, I feel like I *did* know him. Although he was painfully shy, his DNA is linked with mine and so, even still, is an invisible frailty. His shoulders were always slumped over, but nonetheless, the memory of him somehow holds me up.

9

Alpha Females in Separate Cages

Bright-eyed and bushy-tailed, I began at UC Berkeley as a double major in English literature and fine arts. Although there were thousands of Asian American students, there were just a handful in the English department then, and even fewer in the art department. But that wasn't why my social life was nonexistent. I was just naturally kind of a hermit and spent most weeknights in my apartment doing homework and watching *Jeopardy!*

I still remember the time when the TV show was having "college week." I was glued to the set because I was really hoping they'd have a contestant from UC Berkeley. One evening I fixed my usual dinner of champions, Top Ramen with the "Oriental" flavor pack, and sat down expecting some rousing entertainment provided by Alex Trebek and my fellow college-level scholars.

Now, whether there was an actual contestant from Berkeley I do not recall. The thing that sticks in my mind after all these years was that there was an Asian female participant, and she was so enamored of the white boy opponent to her left that she tanked horribly, and her demise left me seething with anger and disbelief.

I don't remember which college had to shamefully claim her as its own, but all the contestants wore sweatshirts with their school names emblazoned on the front, and in my faulty, snarktacular memory, her sweatshirt read RICE. Honestly, at first I thought she was cute. I had high hopes that she would prove to every TV-watching family in America that Asian women are a force to be reckoned with. She had a perky, bobbed hairdo and looked smart, which is to say, she looked Asian. At first glance, I thought she must have believed her right side was her more photogenic, because during the entire game her head was turned toward the left. However, what became quickly apparent was that she was all goo-goo eyes for the white guy on her left with whom she had chummy rapport. Between each of Alex Trebek's questions in answer form, she made chatty little comments to Lover Boy, constantly tossed her hair, and winked like she was plagued with an embarrassing facial tic.

I could accept that she was a boner, I mean a goner, for this guy. However, the thing that made her behavior completely unacceptable was that she was losing. LOSING. An Asian brainiac nerd was losing. Can you believe that? And she was not just lagging behind by a few hundred points, but rather, she had no points at all. Alex would fire off a clue, and when White Boy would hit the buzzer first and answer correctly, she consistently gave him a little high five or a fist bump as if to say, "Sweet!"

Okay, I thought. Convivial relations with the other contestants, and joshing familiarity. That's so college! Right. But after the third or fourth time it happened, and even the sixth time, I was starting to get pissed. Where was her Asian competitive instinct? Seriously, she was letting him win, and she seemed happy about it. I wanted to shout at the TV, "Hey, RICE girl! Get ahold of yourself!" After a while, even the White Guy started to look a little peeved. He gave her a look like, "Um, could you please stop touching me cuz my girlfriend back at Texas A&M is probably watching and also, uh, you're kinda creeping me out."

Meanwhile, in my darkened, dusk-just-turned-to-night apartment with my uneaten bowl of ramen, I was furious. She was Asian, and what the hell was this? If she had been any other ethnicity, I would've just laughed and thought she was a regular-variety dope. But no. Something simmered inside me until I just couldn't take it anymore. All by myself, watching a game show in the dark, I yelled, "CRUSH HIM!"

But she did not. Crush him, that is. It seemed to me that she should have been genetically preprogrammed to demolish any opponent under academic circumstances. But no. Every time the guy answered correctly, she beamed with pride.

C'mon, woman! I'm as romantically deluded as anyone, but if I was on freaking *Jeopardy!* representing my college and the entire Asian American population, I sincerely hope I would self-censor my burning desire to rub myself all over Hunky Boy. Where were her priorities? First win a million dollars, *then* you can hump his brains out . . . LATER. Offscreen, okay? In the privacy of the network green room.

But instead, Asian Girl lost miserably, and when the competition was over, White Guy walked off the platform like she didn't even exist, and she was the one who ended up getting crushed. I wanted to feel bad for her, but I didn't. My Oriental-flavored Top Ramen was cold and so was I. I felt betrayed and disgusted. Poor RICE. What an effing idiot.

After all these years, I still remember watching that episode of *Jeopardy!* Seeing an Asian American female my own age competing against our peers gave me high hopes, but my expectations were dashed. I wanted that girl to represent the best part of me, but I ended up resenting her, that stranger. I wanted her to win above all else, as if she stood for me and every Asian person in the world. I didn't recognize her individuality, her awkwardness, or her humanity. She was just a regular girl whom I was so ready to reflect me, but since she lost, I put her out of my mind. I was eighteen and was searching for camaraderie, even on TV, I suppose.

Actually, I was looking for female friendship in real life, too. But all my friends had longtime boyfriends, and I was the perennial seventh wheel. I was everyone's sherpa, holding coats and wallets when my pals hit the dance floor or went to sweet-talk free beers from the Bear's Lair patio known as The Cage. I was the dork-ass nonblonde. The Chinese one.

Even as my white friends regaled me with tales of drunken parties where Everclear punch was mixed in gigantic plastic garbage bins, I simply regarded them with curiosity. I felt separate from them. I was glad they were having fun, but I did not consider that kind of fun to be available or right for me. My fears about embarrassing my family or, worse, getting a B on the following day's test kept me from any and all festivities.

I felt like a Chinese fighting fish in a small, confined fishbowl. Additionally, when I spotted other Chinese American women on campus, I imagined that we gazed at one another from inside our individual fishbowls, the view distorted by the imaginary glass and water. As we looked at one another without talking, maybe we alternately saw each other and ourselves smaller or bigger than we really were.

In retrospect, my childhood and teen years hadn't much prepared me for female friendships. As my Chinese and American sides were in constant struggle for dominance or equality, my personality had never developed in such a way that I could attain any level of social popularity. All my time was spent in pursuit of straight As or at Chinese school where I felt like an outsider. In the meantime, I hadn't ever learned how to "be myself," let alone how to be a good friend.

I think it's easier for Chinese parents to push for the tangible results of top grades rather than to encourage their children to pursue close relationships. It may not be until much later that social awkwardness rears its pimply head. And by then, the subtle hierarchy and clues to the kingdom might simply further elude a nearsighted brainiac. For me, competition for grades trumped fun and friendship, and that pattern began early. I felt close to neither Chinese nor non-Asians, with only my A pluses and test scores to offer cold comfort.

No wonder I was all alone at night watching *Jeopardy!*

And I wonder, is this when the combination of high achievement and feelings of isolation takes the next step into Tiger Personhood? When one doesn't get close enough to anyone to develop sympathy, empathy, or bonds of friendship, it's easier to stay inside the ever-tightening walls of that locked Chinese box.

The Tiger enclosure is a lonesome cage. It's a form of self-imposed solitary confinement. And if I could go back in time and talk to my younger self, I would say, "Honey, let's not all be alpha females in separate cages."

10

Show Me to the Foxes

Once when I was a little kid, it was a windy day and I said, "Look, Mommy, the clouds are moving." My mom said, "No, they're not." I'm sure she was preoccupied with whatever millionth thing she was doing. But there I was, my insistent four-year-old self. We went back and forth for a long time: the clouds are moving, no they're not, yes, no, they are so moving, I said they aren't . . .

It was an aha moment. I was looking up at the sky and watching with my own eyes as the puffy clouds receded into the distance. I became silent, knowing that my mother was wrong. What insanity was this? How could my mom be wrong when I was still just a little kid? It was my first lesson regarding life being a game that moves as you play.

Folks who haven't been paying attention to the power shift

that has brought the East to the forefront are like clueless adults who haven't noticed that the clouds are constantly moving.

Meanwhile, Asian Americans are up and running, and it's GAME ON. We used to be viewed as the model minority. Call us what you want, but we're breaking out of that mold, too. We're not waiting for approval. We're not the droids you're looking for. You don't need to see our identification. Go ahead and think of us in some kind of old way, as last year's model, but we've moved on.

In fact, we are grown up. Maybe we've got children of our own now. So even if we were willing before to not want better for ourselves, from now on, all that hot mess that we endured as kids just ain't gonna cut it. Hybrid life is the wave of the future, whether anyone likes it or not. We have to live in the in-between times, between the blurred borders of East and West, Tiger parenting and vulnerability, between running fast and enjoying the stillness.

Without our knowledge or consent, the world sees us in many different ways: academic cyborg, materialistic princess, dragon lady, or Hong Kong bar waitress. Often, we are defined as "other." But to us, we're not an "other," we're just us. We are kind people, dutiful daughters, good friends, hard workers, or maybe emerging artists. Maybe we're finding our way, trying on new ways of being, or defining ourselves by comparing ourselves to others. Or maybe it never even occurred to us to be, or not be, what other people projected onto us. What do we want for ourselves?

We are not fixed constellations. We are constantly morphing, changing our ambitions and desires, figuring out what we want, and mashing it up. We have the right to evolve any way we want, at any time we want. The sky is moving all the time, and even supernovas explode. Then where are you, Superstar? You're in a black hole. So keep moving cuz ya don't wanna get sucked into a dark, dead zone and find you can't escape.

And how, exactly, are we going to carve out our identity in this in-between time, between expectation and reality? How will we manage not to get pulled toward the dark side, that is, a life by default that was never of our own choosing?

By being shape-shifters. We can be what we want to be, but are often many things at once: loyal daughter, workingwoman, athlete, caretaker, stone-cold fox. We can be all these things in one day, changing from one type of person to the next, soft one moment, competitive the next. Throughout these changes, inside we are always ourselves, but we keep that hidden from view. Inside is where we live, where the alchemy happens.

I am referring to women and our myriad opportunities and responsibilities now, but even in ancient China, women were perceived as shape-shifters. Men were believed to be fixed in nature, and not fluid like women. Male "yang" energy was threatened by too much female "yin," which is often described as watery, and hence women were sometimes portrayed in tales as eels, or water snakes.

In stories from the Ming Dynasty, there were legends of "fox fairies," beings that appeared in the form of women who were really tricksters with half-animal bodies. Men could be married unknowingly to fox fairies who stole into bed at night with animal prowess. During the day, however, the wife would never be seen without clothes. Why not? Because she was hiding her fox tail, of course! And further, a great part of the allure of bound feet was because women were seen as enchantresses, who were these half-fox beings. The foot as a deformed "hoof" was profoundly enticing. Bound feet were a tradition to keep women at home, but they also caused the hobbled gait that was perceived as attractive. The "fox feet" necessitated a swaying movement, all the more appropriate for a woman who was thought to be changeable and poorly tamed. Through the nationwide practice of foot binding, the fear of women's fluidity and threat of independence was made into physical reality. By this torturous, centuries-old tradition, you could keep your sexy beast at home.

So I say let's turn this ancient idea of women as werecreatures into something that works not against us, but for us. Remember how in *Crouching Tiger, Hidden Dragon* the villainess is Jade Fox? She was a trickster, and no one could catch her. She was a little old lady who killed the greatest warrior of them all, Li Mu Bai (actor Chow Yun-Fat). Well, Jade Fox (actor Cheng Pei-pei) was also the one who expertly instructed Jen (actor Zhang Ziyi) in the ways of martial arts, and besides, she only became evil after some dickhead kung fu master dropped her like a hot potato. So I say, add a little Jade Fox to your life. (And throw in a little jade jewelry while you're at it.)

I think of Steve Martin and Dan Aykroyd playing the two Czechoslovakian brothers in the *Saturday Night Live* skit. They yell, "Show me to the foxes!"

And we are foxy because we have to be. To have room to breathe, we've learned to move through the crevices, and take advantage of the in-between times. I do all my best thinking between dishes and laundry, between dinner and bathtime. And that's not because I wouldn't love to have an office, but rather by necessity. Who has a four-hour chunk of time to herself anymore?

I love the shape-shifters on *True Blood*. I'm sure a lot of women who are fans of that show have imagined themselves turning into a panther to escape modern life's humdrum routines. We can escape by watching shows with hotties who turn into werewolves (Hello, Alcide!), but maybe the idea resonates with us because we ourselves are already a hundred different things to a hundred different people and are constantly transforming our own selves to accommodate others. We make breakfast, send the kids off to school, go to work, call our parents, dress like sirens, and act like poker-faced CEOs. As the old perfume ad used to say, we "bring home the bacon, fry it up in a pan. And never never never let you forget you're a man!"

Lady, we're shape-shifters, all right. We move swiftly through life on our thankfully unbound fox feet. We are tricksters every day because we trick ourselves into feeling like we can do it all; we trick people into thinking we are unhurt inside. We keep our true selves hidden in the cave of our silence. Am I at least a little right? Let's pierce through the idea of perfection with an invisible needle. I know we can do it all, but why should we, all the time, every day? Let's take some time for ourselves.

And last, if you feel like you are stuck in a routine, or a job, or with family duties that you just can't abandon, remember that the ultimate shape-shifter is the phoenix. She is a mythical bird who incinerates herself, then rises from her own ashes. She rises again and again, no matter how often she has previously burst into flames. In Chinese art, the phoenix represents the empress. On textiles and porcelains given as wedding gifts, the dragon represents the husband, but the bride is a phoenix. Even in ancient China, it seems, they knew a woman would need to repeatedly rise from her own ashes.

11

The Garden of Perfect Brightness
Resides Within You

What we need is emotional rescue.

You can get straight As your whole life. You can graduate from high school at the top of your class, go to college, and earn a master's degree or doctorate. You can get a job. You are very good at following the rules, but maybe inside you feel nothing but emptiness.

Chinese thinking is very practical. No one asks you questions about your emotions. Or if they do, it's very direct, and impatient, like, "What do you have to be sad about?"

"What for, this therapy?"

"Why you need to talk?"

Maybe you don't have the vocabulary or terminology to talk about your feelings because you've never developed the language for it. Frankly, it's easier to never even have this conversation with yourself. It is common to busy oneself with all the tasks of living rather than ask about the source of the melancholy. When there is such pressure to succeed, it seems reasonable that one's time is better spent studying or taking care of little brothers instead of moping around and pondering the meaning of existence.

However, this reflection is exactly what's missing in the life of the average Chinese American. There is no sitting around and looking at the sky. After all, where is the practical justification in that? Chinese people may value education, but it's not necessarily for its own reward. In feudal China, passing the scholarly exams was the only way to secure a financial future.

I think Chinese Americans are in a major identity crisis. After all, how do you know who you really are if up to this point in life you've been existing for the needs of all others—your parents, siblings, and grandparents? You've acted according to *their* wishes for you, to make sure someone else doesn't lose face. But what about your own face? You don't even know what it looks like.

Your hours and days have never been your own. Your reputation is not your own. Even your face is not your own. As you go through the motions of living, a lot can get accomplished through an overwhelming sense of duty, added to a fear of failure, and fear of disappointment. Unlike Americans as a whole, I don't think Chinese Americans have ever had their turn-on-tune-in-and-drop-out moment. What would happen if we did?

Most Chinese Americans don't have room to dream because so much achievement, and hence financial success, is expected of them. Not many Number One Sons or Number One Daughters are storming the gates of creative writing programs, let alone turning on, tuning in, or dropping out.

Who has time to write about his or her feelings? They're busy studying, or they're busy working, or they live in an apartment with eight other people, five of whom are their younger siblings who require care and attention. It's only the one or two kids at the bottom who will have time to entertain delusions of grandeur about their silly little aspirations; they are the ones who will have time because the older siblings will have taken the brunt of the parents' strict rules. The eldests can then resent the youngers, and we youngests will wonder what their freaking problem is.

I'm the third born and the only girl. I wasn't Number One, and I wasn't a boy. I was pretty much there to do the dishes and not get in the way. When no one is paying much attention to you, maybe that gives you room to dream. If you're not expected to talk much, that frees you up to listen to everything going on around you. No one thinks you are paying attention. If you are left alone in a room with a stack of paper and pens, and if all anyone wants is for you to not make any noise, well, I say make your own noise in your head. Then write it all down.

In Chinese culture, feelings and writing about them are considered indulgent, especially with a cultural tradition that doesn't promote carrying on like an emotional leaky faucet. If you dare to be unhappy, you're just supposed to throw yourself down a well and be done with it.

Well, forget that.

Have you seen that Catherine Zeta-Jones movie from 1999, *Entrapment*? All I remember is the ad with her beautiful derriere slithering between the trip wires as she eludes a high-tech alarm system for the heist of the century. Whether we like it or not, we gotta be like that gorgeous butt, maneuvering between the laser beams that are the lines that other people have drawn to entrap us.

And for us, what is the heist of the century? We've got to pare down and bring only what we can carry. Anyone else's antiquated ideas of who we are or what they want us to be must be left behind. To go in undetected, we'll need inner strength, poise, and trust in our own abilities. The heist, the big one to end all other jobs, is to take back our dignity, our confidence, and the way we define ourselves.

These abstract, enormously valuable treasures are buried deep inside each of us. They are already ours and are more precious than the contents of any plundered imperial Summer Palace, that Garden of Perfect Brightness.

12

Love, Chinese American Style

There used to be this show on television called *Love, American Style*. During a jaunty little jingle, the credits rolled and showed snippets of happy-go-lucky shenanigans, like skirts blowing up and pants falling down. Tee hee. My husband says that, as a five-year-old, he used to watch the fireworks at the end of the program and feel so giddy that he was convinced that he, too, was actually in love.

For me, growing up in a Chinese household, it never occurred to me that I might someday participate in a *Love Boat*–type of romance or have a *Fantasy Island*, *Charlie's Angels* kinda life. Actually, I didn't realize until I just typed those words that Aaron Spelling is the one who ruined my worldview. No Chinese people on those shows, EVER!

The history of Chinese romance, what do you get? You get married off to a Gold Mountain man while you're in Guangzhou and he goes off to find treasure in California. So while you're standing at the altar, you're tied with a ribbon to a rooster who stands in your husband's place. Or your parents have made a deal with a matchmaker to sell you off to a family down the road when you're only three years old. Of course, these are old world stories. But things aren't that different now. Even my parents joke about my daughter, Lucy, marrying their friend Gene's grandson, Thaddeus. The older generation's utter Chineseness cannot keep them from doing this thing that seems so natural to them: matchmaking, for better and worse.

As for me, everyone always wants to know how I met my husband, Rolf. People were especially interested after I wrote *The Dim Sum of All Things* and pointed out the phenomenon of white men who only date Asians. I called them Asian Hoarders and said they were large mammals in tube socks who tempted victims into their lairs with Drakkar Noir cologne and paralyzed us with saliva like neurotoxic slime. But for the record: Rolf is not an Asian Hoarder. He never had an Asian girlfriend before me. He is, in fact, a large mammal who does own tube socks, but there is no neurotoxic slime involved.

We met in a Chaucer class at Berkeley, so you get a sense of how we're a match made in nerd heaven, complete with the sound of our eyeglasses clicking together when one of us tries to move in for a kiss. I liked him first, but he didn't think of me "that way," so I immediately wanted to destroy him. When I grill him now, he says it wasn't like that. He says, "I just didn't know you liked me. And you were so young." It's true that I was eighteen and he was already twenty-five, and in college that's *old*, man.

But I *liked* his old-manliness. I was attracted to his lack of interest in video games, the fact that he didn't wear stupid Bobby Hill–esque shorts, and his devotion to learning Middle English. Doesn't that just sound dreamy, ladies? Best of all, he was really kind. In a realm where jackass style was the norm, his manner, warmth, and lack of pretense stood out. By then Rolf had already been supporting himself for eight years, so compared to the other embryos at Berkeley, he was already a man, and he was refreshingly competent.

But what was this? He was so clueless it hurt. I was constantly asking him if he knew what time it was, or what he'd thought of last week's reading, and the lummox would launch into a ten-minute monologue about how fantastic "The Miller's Tale" was. Good Lord. I wouldn't have minded him droning on if he would only take his clothes off at the same time. I was patient for several weeks, maybe even the whole semester. However, when he didn't catch the clue bus after a while, I lost interest. "Wife of Bath"? Fascinating, numbskull.

That was my first year in college, but it was his last, so we didn't see each other again for a long time. About five years later, I was at a movie theater with friends when I spotted him walking down the aisle just as the lights were dimming. I know this sounds somewhat implausible, but he's actually really easy to spot. He's a tall redhead with skin so pale he practically glows in the dark. Which came in pretty handy, otherwise I might never have seen him. We said brief hellos before getting shushed, and we somehow managed to signal to each other that we'd meet out in front after the show ended.

Appropriately enough, the movie was *Singles*. When it was over, my friend Bryan and I walked out of the theater and saw Rolf in all his near-albino glory glowing there under the marquee with his friend Gerry. Rolf and I exchanged phone numbers, and after some small talk, we walked off in different directions.

Anyway, so get this miracle: he called me *two days* later, which is a world record when it comes to dating. We made a plan to go out to dinner that weekend, and a few days later when I showed up at his apartment I was happy to find that it was impeccably clean. From there we set off to walk to a nearby restaurant, and on the sidewalk in front of his place he said, "Would it be okay if I put my arm around you while we walk to the restaurant?"

My goodness. That was so wonderful and old-fashioned that I thought we were two leotard-clad midgets in a black-and-white movie embarking on a whirlwind circus romance. I said yes, and off we went.

After dinner we returned to his apartment, and I'm so glad to say that he wasn't one of those guys who shuffled his feet and waited for me to do everything. He said, "Do you want to watch TV?" and I replied, "Okay." So then he turned on *The Simpsons* and promptly pulled me down onto the bed.

Excellent, Smithers.

In the following months, Rolf and I spent a lot of time together, having fun without a lot of money. We walked in Golden Gate Park, collected sand dollars on Ocean Beach, went on road trips, and generally just goofed around.

And as weird as it sounds, I had never just goofed around. It hadn't occurred to me that having fun was something that could come naturally. Before, "having fun" was just one more thing I had to make time for, like studying. I did not look forward to the effort it always seemed to require. But with Rolf, I discovered that having fun wasn't that bad, after all.

Previously, I had felt vague satisfaction when I was winning or achieving something, but what was this new madness? Being content by just hanging out was a freaking revelation. We swam in the American River, made yummy sandwiches, spent time reading, and watched the finest movies his noncable TV could provide. Several months into our relationship, I was sitting on the futon in Rolf's apartment, watching *Kindergarten Cop*. It was then, strangely, that I came to the slow, sinking realization that maybe I was in L.O.V.E.

What the hell is wrong with me? I thought. *I'm sitting here watching this crappy movie, and I'm actually feeling pretty good. I am not even* doing *anything. Why do I feel not just good, but, um,* happy?

It was a very disturbing feeling. Honey Pie was in the kitchen making us milkshakes, and I felt as content as I'd ever been.

So naturally my dad tried to bust us up. He took me to a Chinese restaurant and said, "You've got to stop seeing him. He's too old."

I said, "Aren't you eight years older than Mom?"

"That's different."

"No, it's not."

"Yes, it is."

I'm not sure if what my dad meant to say was that Rolf wasn't Chinese. If he did, he didn't go there. From then on, he took the high road, which was silence. My mom, on the other hand, didn't take the high road.

The Reamer sort of lost her mind and yelled, "What are you doing? You're no better than a prostitute!"

Love you, too, Mom.

Obviously at her wit's end, she deployed her youngest sister, Deanna, to talk to me. My aunt picked me up in her dazzling, two-tone Mercedes-Benz that she has since totaled and told me several things:

1. If I didn't drive a Mercedes-Benz by the time I turned thirty years old, I was a complete loser.

2. I shouldn't be with one guy, I should "screw around" while I still could.

3. I should break up with him so that she and I could party.

You know, thanks, Auntie, but I don't really want to drive around in your Benz and party with you. Just wanna stay home with my lumbering albino and watch *The X-Files*. But thanks, anyway!

Thankfully, my brothers were on my side. What was not to like about Rolf? He could throw a football, play golf, and talk sports statistics for hours. Many, many hours. And to them, that was a good thing. Sure, he drove a crappy Sentra, but at least he knew to wear long pants and a long-sleeved shirt to dinner to meet my parents. Heck, he even cleaned the bread crumbs off the tablecloth with *his own crumber* that he brought along in his pocket. Do you know what a crumber is? It's that little metal thing that waiters use to comb the detritus off the table, and I never knew any regular person who carried around one of those things. What a freak! He was my freak.

Nowadays, my parents really don't like to acknowledge how shortsighted they'd been. He vacuums the cars, digs ditches for them, helps put the Christmas lights on the roof, and does all the other tasks that no one else wants to do. He shucks all the oysters, and cracks the Dungeness crab at dinner, then cleans up all the guts and stinky stuff. When my brother's Australian Shepherd got skunked on Christmas Eve, it was Rolf who took a shower with the dog and cleaned her up. When another pet bolted into the forest on a rainy night, it was Rolf who went after him. At a restaurant where there was no elevator, he carried my grandmother up two flights of stairs, aluminum walker and all, since she refused to let go of it and no one could wrest the cumbersome contraption from her iron grip. And yet another time, Rolf unloaded countless crates of decorations and beverages for my brother's wedding by double-parking several cars in succession in Chinatown in a torrential downpour. You would have thought he was a seasoned valet at Trader Vic's. All these examples serve to illustrate how Rolf will do all that needs to be done. He might be sweating like a pig, but he would never make you feel like he wasn't happy to help you. He is the ultimate Chinese son-in-law. Except that he's so white he's almost see-through.

On the upside, after seventeen years of marriage, my husband's name has finally been changed. When my relatives used to see him at Chinese banquets, everyone would say, "Who's that white guy?" But after so many years of seeing his nonblack head in the crowd, now they just say, "*There's* that white guy."

Interestingly, although my parents had had their doubts, it was my grandma Lucy who was always very enthusiastic about Rolf. Maybe because she had survived bombs falling on her head in China, she knew some things weren't worth getting upset about. She said to me once, "He is very . . . refined."

"Refined?" I sort of wanted to laugh. She made it sound like he drank fine wines with his pinkie in the air.

"Yes. His mother is teacher so he is very refined."

Okay, Pau Pau, if you say so. I wasn't going to dispel any good things she thought about him. She added, "It okay that he not Chinese. You are in love, so it okay."

She was completely nonchalant, and unconcerned about Rolf's whiteness. He had mopped her kitchen floor so she was all good with him. After our little chat, she sat with an unconcerned look on her face, and just went back to watching *Gunsmoke*.

And the rest is history. When the family matriarch gives a thumbs-up to your kind, sweaty, pastel-hued primate, your parents and party-loving auntie just have to shut their yaps.

13

Grandma Lucy on the Page

After graduating from UC Berkeley, I was a butterball bred for high achievement, but I didn't have any idea how I was going to get where I wanted. I held a series of jobs, including five years as a museum bookstore clerk, a year as a high school admissions officer, and six months as a customer service representative at Levi Strauss & Co. I'd always wanted to be a writer and thought a parody called *Wage Slave Luck Club* might make a million dollars. Nonetheless, despite a yearning for a more artistic life, I didn't know how to commit myself to writing while simultaneously earning a living. It was easy to tell myself I was too busy to write. A person could go on for years telling herself that.

But in February 2000, my grandma Lucy died. I was afraid that I would too soon forget how great she was—so kind, quirky, and matter-of-fact. So I started writing little remembrances of her. I wrote little stuff like how she picked her teeth behind one cupped hand and how she'd sometimes just laugh in someone's face when she knew they were full of hot air. Because she was the essence of real, all-encompassing love in my life, I wanted to do her memory justice by recalling her details with clarity and authenticity. My writing that came from thinking about her was something I finally felt was truly honest, not boring or phony. I didn't want to be lazy about remembering her. I wanted to get it right. I was writing about my grandmother, the original Lucy. She was my only Lucy, before my daughter.

I didn't know then that the paragraphs I was writing would become my first book, *The Dim Sum of All Things*. I found that having one idea led me to another, and then another. I just kept going. I told myself I didn't need to know *where* I was going, but it was just important to *keep* going. I didn't have it all planned out.

So I wrote about her in all the in-between times of my life. Back then, my husband was in graduate school, and while he studied, at home I would write just a paragraph or two between doing dishes or folding laundry. I was an office manager at *Mother Jones* magazine, and I jotted down ideas when I was on my fifteen-minute break at work, or even when I was on the bus, scribbling two-word phrases on my Muni transfers.

Frankly, my life greatly resembled that of the book's main character, Lindsey Owyang. I was a receptionist and office manager whose creative bursts at work were relegated to posting pithy threats on the vending machine about not leaving Diet Cokes in the freezer to eventually explode all over the frozen packets of tofu burgers.

In between unjamming the copier and fulfilling the sandwich needs of my superiors, I harbored my secret wish of becoming a writer:

> In the middle of the night Lindsey awoke and could not get back to sleep. She felt restless and hyperawake, as if she had dreamed something thrilling but could now not remember no matter how hard she tried to conjure the dream back. She flipped out of her pink sheets and grabbed her Chococat notebook and poised a pen above the page, willing herself to remember.
>
> It was times like these that Lindsey knew she wanted to be a novelist, but the more she tried to put words down on paper, the only thing she could visualize was the ink drying up inside the pen's cartridge.
>
> From her vanity she gazed out the window at the night sky that was dark and inky, but clear. She felt as if she were the only one who might at this very moment be noticing that the Financial District now lay perfectly still like a geometric pack of stars and galaxies that floated against dark blue glass. She stared for a long time at the impersonal city view, a night skyline of baby supernovas that burned its image in her head like a silent film she had watched long ago.
>
> For a half an hour Lindsey sat wide awake. Eventually she did begin to get sleepy again, and she accepted the gentle pull that drooped her eyelids like velvet curtains. She slipped back under her blankets, and as she lay her head against the pillow, her aspirations, like loose rocks in the caves at Ocean Beach, washed back

into a crevice of her mind where they would have to
wait, dormant until the next wakeful night.

That part of Lindsey Owyang's character was me, and in retrospect, I recognize now that my real motivation to write a novel began when I started to write about my grandmother. And although I hadn't consciously realized it, apparently I had a lot to say about being Chinese. Having spent so many years trying to identify myself without the Chinese thing, interestingly, the themes of identity and feeling caught in the middle of two cultures was exactly what ended up propelling me.

Every day it became clearer to me that I needed to write a book about being Chinese American. I actually felt sick to my stomach sometimes, nauseated by anxiety and ambition. At Browser Books on Fillmore Street I once saw Jade Snow Wong's *Fifth Chinese Daughter* on the shelf and had to run out and immediately go to the bathroom next door at Peet's Coffee. When going to a bookstore spelled immediate bowel problems, I knew I needed either a writing career or a lifetime supply of Pepto-Bismol.

At night I would sneak out of the bedroom as Rolf slept, and I'd write stuff in the kitchen. I wrote descriptions, small paragraphs, single sentences, or single words that happened to be on my mind that day. It was *something,* and that something was better than nothing. I told myself it was okay not to have a master plan, or even an end result in mind. I remember one night I just got out of bed and wrote down some stuff I was remembering about my grandmother:

One time I accompanied Pau Pau to Chinatown to buy
groceries. I went to her apartment but she wasn't ready

yet. I found her in her room standing in her high-waisted granny underwear and a long-sleeved silk undershirt. She pulled on a pair of Jordache jeans and a T-shirt that said FOXY LADY, which my aunt had given her as hand-me-downs from her disco days. Pau Pau topped off the outfit with a polar fleece vest and her favorite quilted jacket.

Pau Pau wore her salt-and-pepper hair in a bouffant. It used to be as big and poufy as Angela Davis's afro in the 1970s, but now her perm hovered about three inches from her scalp, bringing her height to just about five feet tall. After lacing up her Famolares, she went to a nearby chair and reached into the pockets of her previous day's pants, which were draped over the back. She pulled out fistfuls of hundred-dollar bills and stuffed them into the pockets of the pants she was wearing.

"You shouldn't carry that much cash with you," I said.

"What's big deal?" she asked. "Is just mah-jongg money."

I had no idea how or when I was going to use this description, but I felt the need to remember it. I suspended judgment and told myself not to worry about the outcome. It was many months later that I incorporated these paragraphs into a scene with Lindsey going shopping with her grandmother. But if I had never written this little passage, maybe I never would have gotten started. And if I hadn't first taken those small steps in writing remembrances of my grandmother, *The Dim Sum of All Things* would not have existed. Years later, when I would do book readings in stores, it was always so flattering when people would say, "The character of Pau Pau was so real. She made the book come alive."

And I owe it to her that my writing life came alive. Growing up in the 1970s with frequent trips to San Francisco's Chinatown, I strolled with my grandma Lucy, my pau pau, under neon signs that crackled with electricity and spelled out IMPERIAL, EMPRESS, COCA-COLA, FAR EAST, CHOW MEIN, and PEPSI. The Transamerica Pyramid rose up from the east of the Financial District, and cable cars click-clacked straight up California Street like the city's own roller coaster. From the same corner you could see pagoda-shaped turquoise and red streetlamps, and lacquered crimson pillars encircled by golden dragons just like the columns found in the Forbidden City in Beijing. But instead of marking the entrance to the Temple of Heaven, these stately embellishments marked the front door to the neighborhood's temple of finance, the Bank of America.

Across the street was a giant cross at Old St. Mary's Catholic Church, and everywhere there were signs in both English and Chinese, a neon peacock, and tourist shops selling kimonos displayed on mannequins standing in elegant poses. None of the mannequins were Chinese; they were all white, like gigantic Barbie dolls. You'd think an impressionable child might be confounded by all the conflicting imagery, the cacophony of sounds resulting from the constant colliding of two disparate languages. What did I see, hear, and experience in that day-to-day, back-and-forth existence between American life and being Chinese? Was it confusing? Horrifying? Outrageous?

No, Kind Reader.

It was fabulous.

14

Misery Is Not a Contest

At my grandma Lucy's funeral I was a blubbering mess, as were all my mother's sisters. At the end of a Chinese service, it is customary for people to line up and each approach the casket to bow three times to the deceased to pay final respects and to say good-bye. While my aunties and uncle spontaneously engaged in a collective grief circle, through my teary haze I noticed they were all sort of hovering, waiting for my mother to join them. In that horrible moment, they somehow needed her despair to match theirs, to make the intense farewell to my grandmother complete.

Through my own sadness and soggy Kleenex, I watched this scenario unfold. My mother is the least sentimental of her siblings, and I wondered what was going through her sisters' and brother's minds as they wailed with fervor and she stood sad, but still stoic. Their sorrow was real, of course, but was hers any less so because she held in her emotions? Demonstrative outbursts are cathartic, but as I think back now, I wonder if there wasn't also a smidgen of competition going on, as if my mother's siblings were each trying to imply, "Mom and I were the closest, and to prove it, I am going to cry the loudest."

It would be facile to say that my mother's lack of tears was proof of a lack of connection between her and her own mother. However, these days, other facets of my mother's relationship with her own parents come to my mind. In the years of both my grandparents' illnesses and subsequent deaths, it now occurs to me that it had always been my mother who drove them to appointments, got their prescriptions refilled, argued bills on their behalf, completed various chunks of paperwork, and took responsibility for all the tedious, complicated tasks and duties of theirs that would have otherwise fallen through the cracks had she not stepped up. Someone had to be responsible. Most likely, she didn't even want to be the one, but she stepped up to the plate. Over and over again.

My mother was also the busiest of her siblings during that time. As in their earlier years, while her sisters were pursuing pleasures, she, again, was the stalwart. Yes, maybe she was crabby. And difficult. And mad. But as I think back, she was working a full-time job, was still dealing with us three kids as we were each successively leaving the nest, and she was probably going through menopause. But despite these challenges and all her daily duties, there is no way to deny the fact that the Reamer. Got. Things. Done.

So who is to say that crying loudly for two hours at a funeral service is a greater show of love than spending countless weeks, months, and years chauffeuring, tabulating, corresponding, and bookkeeping for one's mother? I see now that even I myself have misinterpreted my mom's lack of showy sentiment. She cared enough and loved enough to do all the crap that no one else wanted to do. She took up the nonglamorous tasks, all the very necessary but mundane, tedious chores like writing to insurance companies and filing tax forms.

And maybe this willingness, this stamina, this recognition of the unsung duties and the meticulous follow-through in completing these tasks has roots in a specific Chinese way of thinking. The humility is actually the strength. She attended to these clerical and practical matters as a show of love and, yes, duty, but didn't expect praise or reward.

When the moment finally did come for my mother to approach the altar to say good-bye to her mother, my pau pau, her siblings cleared a path and waited to see what she would do. They surrounded her, as if to close in on her and squeeze emotion out of her whether she wanted to or not. As I watched from the directly adjacent bench, my mother placed her hand on the casket, emitted the briefest of sobs, like a tiny hiccup, and then just as quickly pulled herself back together. Her sisters were like a chorus waiting for the lead singer's cue, wanting to unabashedly express their collective sorrow. But my mom, even in her grief, would have none of that ballyhoo. After wavering ever so slightly, she sucked in her tears. Her siblings seemed confused, as if their chance to wail en masse had been within such close reach but had now been cruelly denied.

When my mother lost her footing for a moment, several of her sisters grabbed at her shoulders to hold her up. Their fervor just seemed to irk my mom. She steadied herself on the side of the pew and stood up straight. Shrugging off their clinging hands, she said, "I GOT IT."

As the crowd dispersed, various relatives were still crying

their eyes out, myself included. We were wrung out, slumped over, and otherwise incoherent. We were all a collective, tearstained mess, but where was my mother?

I scanned the room, and eventually spotted her, standing next to the funeral director. She appeared sharp as a tack and was going over some paperwork. Oh, that's what my mom was doing. I was glad that someone still had her wits about her. Someone had to pay the bill and make sure the family wasn't getting ripped off.

That was my mother on that very sad day. Looking back, I have gained newfound, albeit very belated, respect for her. My mother is practical. Badass. Even in what must have been her darkest hour.

PART 3

Breaking Out of
the Locked Chinese Box

15

My Mom Loves Fiona Ma More Than Me

 "Hey, Mom. Check it out. My book is mentioned here."

I was holding a local magazine with an earmarked page that referred to my writing, but my mom was too excited about something else to notice it. Nor did she seem to hear me. Instead she handed me a clipping she had carefully cut from the newspaper. It was a picture of California state assemblywoman Fiona Ma.

We didn't personally know Ma. She was not a family friend. But somehow, any Chinese person who has risen to prominence or public celebrity is someone all Chinese people get to take credit for.

"Did you see Fiona's picture in the paper? She got married! Doesn't she look great?"

"Um, I guess."

My mom went on to summarize points from the article, marveling out loud about how Fiona and her fiancé met, and the challenges they might face with her busy schedule as a member of the assembly.

I tried to slink away, not all that interested in hearing about Fiona's nuptials.

"What's wrong? Don't you want to see the picture?"

I ducked into my mom's office near the kitchen. I took a seat at the desk and tried to figure out why I felt so crappy.

I once got a letter in the mail from Fiona Ma. When we lived in the Sunset District, we had painted the outside of our house, and when we pulled off a strip of masking tape from the façade, a portion of paint from the neighbors' house that abutted ours had flaked off with it. The area was small, about one inch by five inches, and we hadn't noticed it.

But our Chinese neighbors did. About a month after we painted the house, we got a letter in the mail from Fiona Ma, who was then San Francisco's District Four city supervisor. The missive requested, in a businesslike manner, that we settle this dispute with our next-door neighbors.

What was she talking about? Our neighbors hadn't even said anything to us, and now we were the recipients of this nice-but-vaguely-threatening letter with an official seal from the City of San Francisco.

It was a big WTF moment, and somehow so typical of our then neighbors. They were a Chinese couple in their fifties, and the only time they ever talked to either of us was when the woman would stop my husband, Rolf, on the sidewalk to scold him because I didn't speak Chinese. To further describe their neighborly ways, they used to leave notes on our car saying not to park in the space between both our houses. They thought they owned that public space on the street. And although they were both able-bodied, they most certainly expected us to reserve that spot just for them. I was irritated enough by the notes they left on our car, but then that official letter in the mail about the house really riled me. Instead of just telling us in person about the small patch of paint, which we would have gladly fixed, they went all insular Chinese Mafia on our asses and got the district supervisor involved.

I wondered if they were related to Ma or knew her parents. Or had they cold-called her office, and we had simply been sent a standard form letter?

Rolf rang our neighbors' doorbell and asked when it would be convenient to fix the paint patch. Obviously, he is so much nicer than I am. I had advised him against it, saying it would be rewarding their backhanded behavior.

I said, "How can you give them exactly what they want when they've gone about the whole thing like such jerks?"

"I don't have time to worry about it. Let me just do it and it'll be done."

So he fixed it. And it was finished. The neighbors were pleased. And I was alone with my seething resentment.

Why did this incident make me so mad? The typical Chinese crappiness of it all caved in my stomach. How many times in my whole life did complete strangers treat me like I was supposed to kowtow to them for the singular reason that we were all Chinese and they were my elders? How many times had I heard in life that I should really speak Chinese? Further, my neighbors' disregard for basic parking rules, and their passive-aggressive way of invoking Ma instead of talking to me like a human being affected me like fingernails screeching across a chalkboard.

And now here was my mom shoving aside the news of my book in favor of reveling in Fiona Ma's dream wedding. Fiona. My old neighbors. My parents. They all seemed to be on some kind of wavelength I couldn't comprehend. A chain of command, a way of doing things, a respect of elders or higher-ups was being adhered to, and I apparently never got that memo because I didn't care about letters from city supervisors, wedding announcements, or the fact that, once and for all, I don't speak Chinese. Not Mandarin. Not Cantonese. Yes, that's too bad. Got it. Filed it.

I just wanted my mom to show a little enthusiasm for my lifelong dream come true, that's all.

Ah. Foolish mortal.

In my parents' house, my childhood home, I let my mom go on a little more about Fiona Ma and her dream wedding. I ate it. I walked away. I didn't know how to express my frustration or my anger. I was a good Chinese daughter and didn't explode.

My parents always ask why I don't stay longer.

In my mom's office near the kitchen there's a corkboard where she has pinned up, along with Fiona's clippings, photos of Other People's Kids. I capitalize the letters of that phrase because they are of supreme importance, apparently. My mom is thorough in recounting who just graduated from Stanford, who is going to be a dentist, and whatnot. Although I don't recognize all of them, my mom sings their praises with regularity. Among these accomplished children of other people, one picture stands out. It's a glamour shot of some girl named Crystal. My mother frequently insists that I know who she is, even though I am certain that I do not.

"Sure, you know her!"

"No, I don't."

"She's our friend's granddaughter!"

"Okay."

"Isn't she pretty? And now she's older, and really, really pretty. You should see her now."

The photo is actually attached to a handle and backed on cardboard. It's a fan. Because, you know, who doesn't need a personal cooling implement for those countless, sweltering days in San Francisco? And if that accoutrement is emblazoned with the pretty face of your pal's granddaughter, I guess it's just a win-win.

My mom talks about Crystal kind of a lot. Crystal, if you're out there reading this, don't you think that's kinda creepy?

Why do Chinese people find it easy to praise other people's kids and yet make their own children feel like we are not good enough? I know it's not just a Chinese thing, but nonetheless, the mind reels. I wonder what primal, cultural, or parental need is getting satisfied by having fantasy surrogate children like Fiona and Crystal. Some might say it's the Chinese tradition not to praise your children or else they will become lazy or will stop striving for the highest level. But more significant, I think, is that Fiona and Crystal can never hurt my mom. Maybe it's safer to love them.

And besides, for all I know, Crystal's parents might have a picture of me on their bulletin board, and Crystal's wondering who the hell I am. Maybe she's thinking, *Dang it! I'm Miss Teen Chinatown so why are there press clippings about this stupid writer all over my mom's wall?*

Who knows. What I do know is that my parents have tons of friends, and all their yearly Christmas cards are all over the house. My mom and dad never throw anything away, so the Christmas cards from past years are taped up, pinned up, and stuck into the corners of cabinets where the glass meets the wood. I have grown up with some of the families and have certainly heard of everyone's accomplishments.

Interestingly though, there are some kids who, mysteriously, are never included in the family photos that we receive. There are disabled kids, delinquents, and ne'er-do-wells. I know they exist because I've seen them from a distance at events, slumped in wheelchairs or moping in the corners, and also I've heard my mom gossiping on the phone about them. But strangely, there is no photographic proof that includes or even vaguely links them to their relatives. Year after year, there is no trace of their existence in holiday photos. They've been "disappeared" by an invisible Chinese shame police.

Chinese people love to project success, and nothing less. If you're unaccomplished, nothing special, or not too easy on the eyes, don't think you can't be deliberately omitted or photoshopped out of the family tree. That's just one more reason to graduate from a top college—so you can be worthy of the Christmas picture!

If you're not an A Plus, with achievements worth bragging about, apparently you just don't make the cut. Your imperfections have been duly noted. You are an inconvenient truth, like global warming. The fact that you are alive and not going to Stanford is a minor annoyance. The holiday photo gets snapped, and the card is mailed to all the friends and relatives, but you have no say in the matter.

And what does *my* parents' holiday card look like? For the

last three years in a row, it has been a photo of my mom and dad, with my daughter, Lucy, in the middle. No one else. There were three different photos, taken on separate occasions. It hardly seemed a coincidence that my husband and I were repeatedly left out of the picture.

When I made fun of the cards, my parents didn't offer much in way of an explanation. All my dad said was, "Well, you weren't around on the day we took the photo. On any of those days, I guess."

16

Nothing Is for Free . . .
Except Breast Milk

When I was pregnant, my spouse and I attended a parenting preparedness class. The teacher asked people in the room to state their names and volunteer tidbits of baby advice for the benefit of the group. We all thought long and hard. Everyone was heartbreakingly earnest. One person advised to hug and kiss your child a lot. Another insisted on the importance of fostering creativity and communication. Someone urged us to help future generations follow their dreams. We all felt warm and fuzzy, snuggling in our collective cocoon of misty-eyed affirmations.

Then a Chinese guy in the group stood up and shouted like a dictator, "You make sure you teach your kids that NOTHING IS FOR FREE!"

The rest of us were stunned out of our soft-focus stupor. He added, "You work hard, or you get what you deserve!"

And that was his baby advice. When he sat back down, everyone had recoiled from their previously open smiles, and some people whispered unflattering remarks about our fellow classmate. But not me. I knew he was just being totally Chinese. He was saying, you want an A on your math test? Then get off your ass. Want a perfect score on your SAT? Then get off your ass. He was saying, work hard if you want a Mercedes, a three-bedroom house with Tara-like pillars, and filet mignon in your belly. Nothing is for free. The unspoken message in his words was, in China you work your ass off but you still get nothing. Here you have opportunity so don't piss it away. When Communists destroy your family and house, imprison you and send your children away from you for hard labor in the countryside, then your Montessori-educated ass will have something to cry about.

So very Chinese.

And he wasn't just talking to the white people. I felt he was talking directly to me. I spent my whole life trying to hug everyone in my family because I was just a sheltered, spoiled, little lovebug. My attempts to rub my chubby face on everybody's tits just made them, well, uncomfortable, to say the least.

Speaking of which, it was just a few months later when a newborn little somebody was doing the same thing to me, that is, rubbing her face all over my boobies, looking for some damn milk.

It was mere hours after I gave birth to a gigantic baby the doctor had dubbed "the Hulk." I was delirious from lack of sleep, a morphine drip, and the fact that a team of doctors had just unzipped my abdomen and removed a nine-pound, eleven-ounce human being from my body. Suddenly, seemingly out of nowhere, it was time for my hospital-appointed training session on how to milk myself. It was then that the lactation specialist entered my room and unceremoniously pulled open my nightgown. "Oh," she said with pleasant surprise, "you have African American boobies."

This struck me as a weird thing to say to a sleep-deprived woman with an intravenous feeding tube, catheter, and no pants on. But that's what she said, right in front of the team of doctors, nurses, and relatives who had all come to fuss and take pictures of Baby Hulk and my zitty, sweaty, bleeding-from-the-crotch self.

The boobie nurse felt me up like a lusty, somewhat clinical sailor, and all I could do was lie there and thank my maker for the morphine drip, compliments of Brown & Toland. I am very modest, you see, and am usually reluctant to whip off my high-school-era minimizing brassiere within the peripheral vision of my best girlfriends or even my own mommy.

Was the nurse saying my breasts were big or small, or a different shape than she expected? Having recently had my gut slit open via C-section, I was still reeling from the sight and sound of my amniotic fluid gushing onto the operating room floor. I was trying to think of a tactful way to apologize to the doctor for drenching his Bruno Maglis with my innards, and I simply was not ready to discuss the racial differences of boobies. Nonetheless, lying there, I wondered whether I needed to give a little speech about how I was proud to be a Chinese American. How my boobs were proud to be Chinese American, too.

She pulled my top open farther so that even the janitor who'd come to empty the trash could see my African American boobies. Watching him carry out a bag that said CAUTION:

BIOHAZARD, I was jarred back to my breast-feeding lesson. The lactation specialist then ordered me to "squeeze it like a hamburger." Breasts aren't even shaped like Whoppers or Quarter Pounders, but I'm a people pleaser, so I tried to do as I was told. I pinched and compressed my flesh without success. In my anguish, I reminded myself that I needed to feed my infant. Bilirubin buildup was threatening to turn my baby the color of a pumpkin, and she was already in the butternut squash spectrum.

So I had African American boobies. Whatever the definition, there ain't nothing ghetto fabulous about cracked nipplage, latching on, or pumping and dumping. Breast-feeding is all fun and games until someone gets an eye poked out with a giant, swollen, thumb-length nipple.

Eventually, like many unsung mothers throughout the ages, I finally did figure out how to get the milk out of my engorged breasts and into the mouth of the Hulk. Nonetheless, as relieved and happy as I was about the mammalian success of my body parts, I was still miffed about the racial misidentification of my rack.

If you have ever been unfortunate enough to sit through the entirety of Steven Spielberg's movie A.I., you may recall that, after all human beings have been extinguished from the planet, aliens revive Haley Joel Osment's bloated robot corpse from the bottom of the ocean because he is the only half-decayed remnant of a creature who has any memory of what real humans were like. In my postpartum delirium, I wondered if I, too, could be revived millennia from now by benevolent aliens seeking a glimpse of African American breasts. Or maybe the aliens would just choose to reanimate an African American woman instead of me, having used their outer space powers to ascertain that my breasticle anomaly wouldn't be worth bringing me back to life because, based on their records, all indications pointed to the fact that in my heyday I was a persnickety buzz-kill.

I still think back to those early days when I was a new mom and figuring out how things were supposed to work. That was almost a decade ago, and when I'm lying in bed next to Lucy now, I am glad we are still close. The other night, she reached across my chest and gave me a squeeze.

"I like your boobies, Mommy," she said, patting them. And at that moment, that was all the cultural reassurance I needed.

17

Tiger Mom's Heart Grew
Two Sizes That Day

"I had never seen anything like it," my husband said. "You were in the recovery room and your mom and I looked through the glass partition and saw the baby swaddled there in the tray. Your mom looked at Lucy with *tears* streaming down her face. She was *crying*. It kind of freaked me out."

Who knew that a blob of joy with thighs like biscuit dough could move my mom to tears? While Rolf counted Lucy's fingers and toes out loud, my mom's face was reportedly, yes, leaking spontaneous tears of happiness.

Of all the family photos in my parents' house, there is only one of my mother as a child. She is standing knock-kneed on an army base in Hong Kong, the expression on her face confused at best. She is about three years old and is grimacing in distress, even as she is held in place by her mother. My grandfather stands confidently alongside them in his U.S. military uniform.

My mother arrived in this country speaking only Chinese and was placed in a lower grade for her age because of her lack of English. Her parents struggled to find housing and work, as she and her older sister navigated their new school and all the different faces and customs they encountered. Money was tight, the foods were unfamiliar, and I can only imagine that my mother did not have a happy-go-lucky childhood.

From the moment my baby was born, my mother expressed such delight in her that at first I was taken aback. For my whole life, my mother never acted giddy, or even a little bit goofy, and there she was, making faces, playing peekaboo, singing, and gently tickling Baby Lucy. Through my daughter's infancy and toddlerhood, my mom held and comforted her, chased and played with her. My mom became both the kid she never got to be and a young mother once again. It seemed that all the things she didn't have time to do with me were made right in this second chance with her granddaughter. My mom could be silly! Who knew?

And I guess this is as good a time as any to say that during those first years of Baby Lucy's life, my mom totally saved my ass. My mother was my rock. Other than my spouse, I trusted no one else to feed, bathe, and take care of my daughter. Up to that point, I had viewed my mother to be pragmatic to a fault, but all her practical know-how in cleaning, measuring, diaper changing, clothes washing, and snot wiping came to my rescue when I was a sleep-deprived know-nothing.

I was adept at many things in life, like how to organize an office of fifty people, how not to get pickpocketed on the bus, how to walk into popular restaurants and get seated quickly even without a reservation, and other urban survival skills. But for some reason I had never had any experience with babies. I didn't have younger siblings or infants around in my household so I had never even changed one diaper before I had Lucy.

People might think a new mother just magically "knows what to do." And all I've got to say to that is, ha ha ha ha. In various jobs I've held for pay, I attended seminars to familiarize myself with computer programs and trained with my superiors to learn the ins and outs of becoming a team leader. However, never in my life had anyone ever clued me in about cradle cap, pinkeye, ear gunk, or cleaning milk out from under a baby's neck. So thankfully, here was my mom, having not been around an infant in several decades, but nonetheless, she was, in fact, the Blob Whisperer. As if she had cared for us babies only yesterday, she miraculously could read the subtle nuances in infant gurgles, hiccups, and squeaks.

I cannot overestimate how comforting it was to have someone around whom I could trust to keep my baby alive. I was in that hysterical, new-mom headspace where I would wake up in the night and hold a small mirror up to the baby's mouth to make sure she was still breathing. The only thing that quelled my all-consuming anxiety was knowing that I could take Lucy to my mother for a few hours in the morning, and she would be safe while I tried to catch some sleep.

My mom accompanied me to the baby's doctor appointments and played bad cop to my good cop when it was time to get shots. She didn't lose her mind like I did when Lucy wailed in fear. Someone had to not be the basket case, and that was my mom. I had never fully understood that being the person who gets things done is a crucial yet unsung position in life. Her pragmatism allowed me to be a mess. Her strength allowed me to flail around like a depressed, weepy, stressed-out mammal in milk-stained clothes. Until I could gather my marbles and come to grips with the fact that my college education and urban life skills meant practically nothing in this new endeavor, my mom was there keeping the baby clean, fed, washed, and happy.

I had always considered my mother to be short-tempered and difficult, and I thought of myself as someone who was affable and accommodating. Weirdly, though, now our roles were reversing. My mom transformed into a more pleasant person as she reveled in Lucy's innocence and sweetness. Meanwhile, I was the one becoming a cranky pants as I dealt with my changing body, new responsibilities, and the realization that old freedoms that I had taken for granted were now suddenly ripped away, never to be seen again.

During my daughter's earliest years, my mother and I spent more time together than we had in two decades. In that time, she became younger and I became older. She reconnected with the playfulness of youth, and I began to understand that becoming an adult meant putting someone else's needs before my own for every meal, shower, snack, clothing change, and need to pee. It was a major learning curve to always think to wash someone else's hands before my own, fix a twisted sock, roll up a sleeve, cut a piece of meat, find a sequin lost in the carpet, or handle any such earthshaking minutiae before even taking a sip of water for myself.

I did not magically "know what to do." As an adult, growing

up continues to be a learning process as I help someone else to grow up. I am grateful that in my early years of motherhood, I had someone in my corner helping to do all the unsung, mundane, immediately crucial work of keeping my daughter fed, comfortable, and thriving.

My mom and I are not exactly chummy best friends. But she was my rock when I needed one. And like I said, she certainly saved my ass. And I will never forget that.

18

Mompetitors, Start Your Engines!

I hadn't fully understood the importance of having a group of friends until I had a baby and started to spend time with other moms. Up until then, I'd had solid friendships with individuals, having forged bonds through school or a mutual love of art and writing. However, when the baby bomb detonated, it created total chaos in my body, brain, and living room.

I am not sure if motherhood levels the playing field or obliterates it as would an underground nuclear explosion. Dirt, weeds, small animals, uprooted trees, and all manner of flying detritus rain down on your head, or at least that's what it feels like. The needs of your deflated body, demanding family, and cuddly, perhaps colicky baby are a whole new minefield that you must navigate. And where once you could walk a straight line to get somewhere, you might suddenly find that the ground has now somehow turned to Jell-O. As a new parent you search for solid footing, only to encounter sinkholes filled with Marshmallow Fluff.

I didn't find immediate camaraderie on playgrounds or in moms' groups. In fact, my first foray into fellow-parent bonding didn't work out so well at all. When Lucy was three years old, I enrolled her in the same tiny tots program I had attended as a child. I hoped that we, as mother and child, would have two tons of fun. I assumed I'd feel at least a little bit like I belonged since, after all, I had attended the place myself, back in the 1970s. Of course, I wouldn't have expected any of the old teachers to still be there, but I at least thought the other parents would be *nice*. But dang if the social hierarchy wasn't bursting with mompetitors with poopie personalities. My childhood playground had now become a gathering spot for Mean Girls with Strollers.

There was a preexisting superclique of redheaded gals, and as they all chatted in a tight circle, I did occasionally rescue some of their boys who were upside down in the sandbox and couldn't right themselves. Or sometimes the boys got stranded on the rickety play bridge, dangling helplessly by their ankles while their moms remained oblivious. I tried to be helpful. I wanted to be liked so much that I even tried to interject into conversation that my husband was a redhead, as if they'd accept me into their group by hair color proxy. But they weren't interested. Not even when I offered to share my organic fake Oreos.

Nor was it a love connection between our offspring. Lucy observed the other children from a safe distance, and when I asked if she wanted to join the other kids, she observed the *Lord of the Flies* melee by the play structure and uttered one scathing word, "Cooties."

There were also two Asian moms at this tiny tots, but they kept to themselves and didn't talk to anyone, not even to each other. Not that they should have immediately been friends because of their ethnicity, but in my petty, competitive mind I hoped and schemed about forming a Super Asian Mom clique that might topple the dynasty of excluding redheads. That was my revenge fantasy, anyway. But when I smiled at them from across the circle as we all sang "The Wheels on the Bus," neither Asian gal smiled back. They both did the little hand movements with looks of complete boredom on their faces. Meanwhile, I tried to at least feign enthusiasm for the sake of my kid.

I unsuccessfully attempted to suspend judgment as I watched the Asian woman with the cropped hair constantly check her phone and the one with the glasses as she frantically texted. They should have been doing the swish-swish-swish motion with their hands, and the swirly wheel thing with their fingers. I wanted to say, "Come on, ladies! This time, with feeling!"

But what I hadn't counted on was that these Asian moms apparently couldn't stand to be doing nothing. And by nothing I mean being mentally present as toddlers all around us drooled and spaced out. They both seemed horrified at the pointlessness of singing songs when the time could have been more effectively used to check in at their respective offices via phone. I watched from a short distance as they each directed focused intensity on their devices and their kids sat like well-dressed lumps on the mats. I wondered, why bother coming to a tiny tots playgroup at all if you're not going to even pretend to spend time with your kid?

With these Asian moms whom I failed to connect with, I definitely got the impression that associating with others here in our modest parks and rec building might risk throwing off their schedules. They each stayed only for exactly twenty-five minutes, then efficiently packed up their strollers and offspring and went off to their kids' next activities. Having once asked each separately where they were off to, I received the curt replies, "Karate and Kid Yoga," and "Level Two Gymnastics and Ballet with Miss Tilly."

I particularly noted the one woman's need to denote "Level Two," lest I mistakenly assume that her kid, who was shorter than the length of my arm, was only a lowly tumbler. In addition, Level Two mom then caught a glimpse of Lucy playing with a leaf and rolled her eyes at me. She grabbed her kid's wrist and pulled her away from us just in case her own daughter might get any bright ideas about remedial leaf exploring, as if that would forever doom her to an entry-level job in the food industry. I just shrugged it off. I'm not one of those moms who thinks getting into Harvard depends on early enrollment in preschool Pilates.

Over time, I did slowly find other mothers with sensibilities similar to my own. The conversations came easily, and we talked about the mundane things that were now a part of our daily lives: making noodles, washing underwear, mopping floors, fighting about boogers, and dirty hair. We laughed about how our brains were turning to mush, but we bolstered one another's morale with adult cynicism while we discussed various toddler TV shows:

"Which guy do you like better on *Blue's Clues*, Steve or Joe?"

"I can't decide between the pinhead or the one who just looks like a mouth-breathing masturbator."

"Bert or Ernie?"

"They're both gay, of course. Hiding together under the Q for Quilt, reading a book, with a big Q for Queen. Ernie, stop spraying me with that hose! 'Doing the Pigeon' sounds like a song Bert learned in San Quentin."

"The Care Bear stare is like spray-on Ritalin—wish I had some of that."

"When Big Bird sings about adoring the number four, does he say 'crashing bores,' or 'trashy whores'?"

I can't imagine that Tiger Moms allow themselves the closeness that results from sharing, because to do so, they'd have to let their hair down. Friendship with other moms comes from admitting mistakes, revealing messy truths, and laughing so hard that you kind of pee your pants a little.

And how can a woman do that if she's still striking that impossible pose of perfection? One-upmanship, comparing your kids' accomplishments, and securing your bragging rights or moral high ground do not bring people closer to you. Those hallmarks of Tiger Moms only serve to keep everyone at arm's length. Ultimately, it's a recipe for even more loneliness.

During Lucy's baby and toddler years, I was glad to have met those few women who helped me feel less alone. Some moms were stricter than others, and we didn't agree on everything, but we enjoyed one another's company without having to feel competitive, which felt good.

That was several years ago now. Back then, I was just starting to find camaraderie, and more surprising, I was getting along pretty well with my very own mother. Nonetheless, in the near distance, or maybe just inside me, a storm was brewing.

19

Iris Chang It

I always suspected there were pitfalls to being a high-achieving Chinese American, but the severity of the dangers really shook me to the core when Iris Chang shot and killed herself.

Iris Chang was a Chinese American writer who was my age and also had a child around the same time my daughter was born. She lived in San Jose, which is very close to San Francisco, so when I saw the headline "Local Chinese American author, 36, found dead of self-inflicted gunshot," for a split second I thought, *Oh, hell, am I dead?*

I stared at the wall, and for a good twenty seconds I pondered the possibility that I might be one of those confused ghosts haunting my own house because I didn't realize I was dead. After poking myself in the leg with a pencil and ascertaining that I was still living in the flesh, I went on to read the devastating news about Chang, a brilliant star whose light was extinguished on an early November morning.

By all accounts, she was the ultimate go-getter, convincing the *New York Times* to let her be a stringer in the Champaign-Urbana area of Illinois when she was still in college. Other students envied her ambition and success, and the author Paula Kamen even described Chang's gumption as a verb, telling her students who longed to accomplish something to just "Iris Chang it."

Chang wrote three books, *The Thread of the Silkworm, The Rape of Nanking,* and *The Chinese in America.* They were all books that any Chinese parent would be proud of. They were scholarly works with no F-bombs, or scenes describing crapping your pants, or plotlines with an underaged Lolita watching a guy spank his monkey. Those classy bits were the cornerstones of my novels. Part of me would've loved to be Iris Chang, but for the most part I knew that Iris had a gift for elegance, while my specialty, apparently, was sweet, lowbrow profanity.

I'm just gonna start referring to her as Iris now, because it feels like we were friends. With each book that she produced, I felt pangs of jealousy. I would take particular notice whenever her name appeared in the news. Ah, look at her shining face, standing there with Bill Clinton. Oh, look, there's her name on the top of the bestsellers list. Gee, look, they're erecting a statue of her in the city of Nanking, China.

It was a friendly envy because I wholeheartedly admired her bravery and her writing, and how she reached back into history to shed a spotlight on the atrocities against the Chinese during World War II. My own grandma Lucy had fled Japanese bombs in China, and she had told her heartbreaking, horrifying stories to me as Chang's grandparents had also done with Iris, so

The Rape of Nanking was especially meaningful to me. And now Iris was dead.

Damn! I always thought Iris and I would have met up somewhere, like at a conference or panel at the library. I had looked forward to the day when I might gush at her like a swooning fan, and we might be able to swap stories about balancing the writing life with raising a kid.

But none of that would be happening. One early morning, Iris left her bed and got in her car to drive a short distance from home to inflict a single gunshot to her own supersmart, beautiful head. All that gorgeous hair, creamy skin, and pretty face I imagined splattered in her own blood on the car seat.

Although she was a stranger to me, it felt like a stab in the heart.

Oh, what if we *had* been friends? Could an acknowledgment of mutual, separate loneliness have made any difference at all? Or maybe a competition between us would have made things that much worse.

I fantasize about how just one association, one person, one more ally could have changed the outcome for Iris. I know this after-the-fact speculating is unrealistic, futile, and perhaps pompous of me, but I imagine the various scenarios still.

Was it really that bad? Couldn't she walk away from her responsibilities, or move to Tahiti? No way. No, no, no. Of course not. Apparently, that's not how Iris Chang rolled. She was the superachieving firstborn child of two superachieving parents (they are both scientists), and when you throw in that Chinese thing . . . well.

Many reasons and speculations abound for what ended Iris Chang—depression, bipolar disorder, her deep empathy for the victims she wrote about, and other theories. The *San Francisco*

Chronicle Magazine wrote a cover story about her, detailing her achievements and her last days and funeral. The article described her husband taking her to Fresh Choice for their wedding anniversary, how she would work nonstop for days, and how she regularly exhausted herself completely.

I read and reread this story and have even saved it all these years, still flipping through it from time to time. I'm not sure how to feel about Iris Chang, her accomplishments, and her death. There's the sickness I feel over her tragic end, and then there are the details we had in common that add a macabre quality. Mostly, though, what pained me and troubles me still about her death is that she was someone I looked up to, who gave me hope and a little bit more courage. I had considered her a better, more respectable version of myself. When someone whom you've always admired can't stand the heat in the kitchen and decides to off herself, what are you supposed to do?

I think about Iris Chang all the time. When I'm tired, when I want to stop writing altogether, or when I need a pep talk, I consider all the ways in which Iris could've been easier on herself. Since I didn't know her personally, I have no firsthand knowledge of her foibles, her intensity, or her work habits. Her being gone and my being alive to wipe up baby barf and write books about interracial dating and preteen, smutty high jinks seemed unfair.

Sometimes when I want to give up everything and not get out of bed, I think of Iris. Not because she would've definitely gotten out of bed, but because I can. I have a chance to write about all these things that happen to me, and somewhere there's someone whom I may never meet and she is reading my books. Maybe my words can make her feel better, or inspire her to be the next writer who makes a difference. We all keep passing the baton to the next person who can tell the truth, and that humble continuity is what we'll need to break apart the abstract wall of Chinese silence that keeps us separate, each alone within ourselves.

20

The Wheels Start to Come Loose

I knew it was time to leave San Francisco when the police shot and killed the tiger at the city zoo. We'd been going there three times a week for the past four years and had just visited the tiger's grotto that very same morning. Lucy and I had spent her early childhood watching Tatiana pace her enclosure. We had crouched dozens of times behind the thick Plexiglas and quivered as she meandered by, six inches away with those white whiskers and clear yellow-green eyes. And now she had died in a hail of bullets on Christmas Day.

As for us, truthfully, we were not doing too well in San Francisco either. Entrenched in those hard years of early parenthood, Rolf and I had divvied up the responsibilities of family life and, as a result, hardly spent any time together anymore. He was working long hours in the school district, and I was watching Lucy and writing my second and third books, *Buddha Baby* and *I Want Candy*. I didn't venture out of the house very often, but when I did, it seemed like everywhere we went, the rage and unhappiness of the world accosted us at every turn. A complete stranger in a Safeway parking lot ran up to me as I balanced my sleeping toddler across my chest while lugging three bags of groceries and screamed at me for not returning my cart to the designated area. On a daily basis, Chinese passersby scolded me for not wrapping Lucy in a sweater and tighter blankets, and once in the Japanese Tea Garden in Golden Gate Park someone called me a "f*cking chink" under her breath as I waited in line for the bathroom.

Before I had a baby, I often jokingly described myself as a freak magnet, meaning that I somehow attracted people's bad behavior, and I do believe it has something to do with looking like a Harmless Asian Girl. Guys walked up to me all the time and said lewd things. On a crowded Muni bus, a man reached over and palmed my ass. Homeless guys made sexual gestures at me frequently. Mind you, none of this crap ever happened if I was with Rolf. It was only when I was alone, or alone with Lucy. If you've ever been a new mom, you know that you find yourself unaccompanied a lot of the time, living your lonely life at the height of your body's and baby's vulnerability.

If I ignored these behaviors, more often than not, I would hear muttered expletives as I passed. If I saw a potentially unsavory character up ahead on the sidewalk and crossed the street, I'd also get an insult hurled my way or at the very least a scornful gaze and wad of spit aimed in my direction. None of this was ever fine with me, but I accepted and endured it as part of city living.

My body had been ripped apart, I wasn't sleeping very much, and I was trying to figure out how to take care of this helpless creature whose wide-eyed stare told me she depended on me completely. Under the strain and complexity of having this new and innocent person, the crass behavior of strangers became unbearable.

Add to these incidents the regular annoyances of city life. Nearly getting killed in the crosswalk as a pedestrian was no joke. Drivers zoomed straight at our stroller all the time, just to stop on a dime and get pissed off if I gave them a dirty look. No one seemed to ever stop at stop signs, and cars turning right against the red light often honked or peeled out inches from my heels if I wasn't moving fast enough for them. Once when I was in the crosswalk with the light in my favor, Lucy's sweater slipped into the street and I stopped to pick it up only to have a turning car come to a screeching halt. I could see the driver inside screaming obscenities at me.

Needless to say, my nerves were shot.

Meanwhile, Rolf was working like a dog. Because he was often one of the only male teachers at the various sites he covered, he was frequently asked to restrain kids, break up fights, and defuse angry parents. Several families were suing the school district, and in some neighborhoods where he worked, violence was prevalent. He'd come home exhausted, and I wouldn't tell him anything that might stress him out further. I didn't mention the off-leash psychotic pit bull that chased me down the sidewalk, and I kept quiet about the skateboarder who barreled down Stanyan Street and nearly knocked both Lucy and me to the ground.

Also, every weekend it seemed we were required by my

family to go to one event or another. So-and-So was having a recital, baby shower, wedding, birthday, you name it. Don't you remember their daughter? Sure you do. You *have to* be there. My brothers would somehow get a pass and avoid going to these events, but because I was the daughter and had a baby for my parents to show off I was always given the hard sell. So we'd end up going to something every weekend, sometimes on both Saturday and Sunday, and then the week would start up again on Monday without much relaxation having happened at all.

Not that we remembered how to relax or would recognize it if it bit us in the rump. Rolf had work reports to write on his own time at home; our toddler required constant feeding, wiping, washing, and entertaining; and I was trying to carve out time and space to write. I could barely scrawl out a grocery list in my sleep-deprived state, and yet my deadlines loomed closer. You've heard the phrase "time marches on"? Well, dishes, diapers, and laundry marched on for us.

We saved time by not talking to each other very much anymore. We knew what we had to do—slog through. And we did slog through. For about five years. And with each passing year, the talking became more minimal. We lived in completely different realms. He was working and trying to soothe overwrought kids and crazed parents, then coming home to write up the status reports under constant threat of the school district's lapsed compliance to federal standards and impending lawsuits. I was writing novels, wiping up yucky things in a world of Elmo and *Yo Gabba Gabba!,* and making organic baby meals churned through a hand grinder and popped into ice cube trays for future single servings.

Within this time, everyone under the sun was also asking

us when we were going to have another baby. Strangers asked me how old I was or told me that I was running out of time. Random people would scrutinize my stomach or actually reach out and pat my postpregnancy tummy pooch and inquire if there was another bun in the oven, hopefully a boy this time. Or else they'd ask when I was going to lose that weight. Someone once even checked out my chest and said it looked like there was still a lot of milk in there.

I pretty much wanted to die.

But instead, I began to act out in other, small ways.

For instance, I tried to steal a Radio Flyer peanut-shaped tricycle. I was foiled by an early-bird parent who showed up at the Walter Haas Playground at seven in the morning with her adorable toddler just as I was plotting to hoist the minitransportation device into the back of my hooptie rust-bucket roller skate of a car. The tricycle had been at the playground for weeks! Someone was bound to eventually take it. Why couldn't that someone be me? I chickened out because of the potential mommy narc, and when I went back the next day to the scene of the near crime, the peanut trike was gone. Someone who was either less of a coward or more of a brazen criminal had beaten me to the punch.

So then I focused my wayward tendencies on people's misplaced wallets.

For about a period of six months, everywhere I went I was finding people's wayward billfolds. Leather, pleather, Velcro, Coach, with checkbooks, credit cards, and stuffed with cash. I found one by the drink machine at the zoo, one on the platform of the nineteenth-century carousel in the park, and several in malls and clothing stores. If the wallet was on the ground, I rolled over it with my secret weapon—a gigantic baby stroller containing my gigantic baby. Ah, the perfect cover. Who would suspect a nice Asian gal with a stroller to be *une* thief *extraordinaire*? I'd hover over the goods and then bend down to pretend I was procuring some Cheerios for my spawn, but instead I'd retrieve the wallet, filled with untold amounts of fabulous cash.

After waffling for a few moments, I always did turn in the wallets to the proper authorities. But why didn't I take the money and run? Mostly because I'm totally vain. Doing bad stuff like stealing money causes guilt and regret that eventually shows up as deep crevices on your face, and then you're one of those people who coulda maybe been almost pretty but is disturbingly hagged out before her time, and who needs that? I can't afford Botox, for criminy's sake.

I don't know why these wallets were scattered around San Francisco for me to happen upon them. But of all morally ambiguous things, stealing money ain't okay, right? That's what I figured after I imagined all the wonderful things I could get on eBay with money that wasn't mine.

Which brings me here. Let's get down to brass tacks, shall we?

We didn't have enough money to stay in San Francisco. Like a lot of people, we were siphoning liquid cash out of our home equity line, hoping to pay off the minimum balances until we won the California Lottery. We were $90K in the hole and had further debt stashed in various 0 percent APR accounts, but they were all coming due and ready to switch over to 29 percent interest rates with fees so numerous that I could only stare at the wall and helplessly, nonsensically ponder the name of the Tubes' lead singer, Fee Waybill. Bills? Fees? No way. Way. Fee Waybill. Waived fees? No way. Way. Fee Waybill. And over and over.

We wuz broke and I was considering morally questionable activities despite my deep fear of Satan.

Something had to happen. We had to break out of our rut. I didn't want to end up dead like Iris Chang or get thrown in the slammer for stealing wallets.

I was a haggard mom with a beautiful baby, but we were slogging through our days. We lived in one of the most dynamic cities in the world, but didn't feel happy. Something had to change.

21

The Mice Go On

Let's just say I was in despair but didn't know it. Maybe it was best not to admit it to myself, because I figured there was no point in complaining. No one wants to hear it when someone talks about her vague feelings of impending doom. If any person noticed me looking dejected and said, "What's your problem?" the only answer I could muster was, "Nothing. Everything's fine."

One weekend, we took a drive up to the Sierra foothills and visited the town of Nevada City. We'd been there several times a few years earlier, before we'd had Lucy, to have lunch and sightsee. This time, while I was browsing in a shop, Rolf waited on the corner in front of a real estate office and absentmindedly scanned the home listings.

"Check this out," he said when I came out of the store. It was a Victorian house nearby, a place that didn't end up being what we needed, but right then, an idea quietly began to germinate.

Later that night, in the darkness, with both of us awake and knowing the other was up but not saying anything, I finally whispered, "What if we moved?"

"You could never leave San Francisco."

"Well, why couldn't I?"

"Could you?"

"You're right. I couldn't."

Variations of this terse conversation popped up for the next few nights. Meanwhile, during the daytime we were consumed with our frantic search for a public kindergarten for Lucy. San Francisco Unified School District uses a lottery system to place students in different schools. You are supposedly guaranteed one of your top seven choices, but we had been through the lottery twice, and neither time were we selected for any schools nearby or that I'd even heard of. There were ten schools in our neighborhood that would have been all right with us. But wanting a school assignment close to a kid's home is treated as a petty, bourgeois request in the City by the Bay. The situation was further demoralizing because Rolf had been busting his butt for the district for six years, but despite his dedication, the impersonal kindergarten placement process continued to dog us.

So on another night, without actually bringing up the question of moving, I said, "Do you want to go up to Nevada City again this weekend?"

Rolf gave me a look. "Okay," he said.

In retrospect, I can only say that maybe when you're about to make a crazy, life-changing decision, like leaving the one home you've ever known, you can only summon the nerve by not thinking directly about it too much or you'll scare yourself out of doing it. So we dropped Lucy off with my parents, and we spent the next few weekends looking at homes in Nevada City.

And why there? It was only three hours away from San Francisco, close enough that we wouldn't feel too cut off, and far enough to feel like my nerves could recover. And it is very beautiful. I feel most comfortable in old places, and Nevada City is one of the oldest in California, and there we would have snow in the winters and hot sunshine in the summer, something I definitely never had in San Francisco.

During those weeks of driving back and forth I did wonder to myself if we were insane to uproot ourselves. We alternated between giddy excitement and cold sweats. I would wake up in the middle of the night and for a few seconds think, *God, I had a horrifying dream that we moved out of San Francisco.* The next day I might think, *Thank goodness we didn't do something stupid,* and then I'd change my mind and say to Rolf, "Why not? People move all the time. We can do it!"

The idea of leaving my hometown and my entire life as I knew it up to that point might sound impulsive, and I admit that it was. The thing I may not have emphasized, though, is the heavy, intense feeling of dread I felt every minute of every day. People could argue that there is crime everywhere, and most car accidents happen within a mile of home wherever you are. Also, it's more likely you'll slip in your own bathtub than get mugged at gunpoint. The general consensus is that you can't let fear rule your life.

But fear was definitely getting the better of me. And it wasn't just because I was a hypersensitive mom with a toddler. I was that, true, but in the last three years, danger seemed to be escalating all around us. Parents at the schools where Rolf worked were choking and shooting each other, a girl was killed three blocks from our home in a case of mistaken identity, and a kid we knew was mauled to death by his family's pet pit bull. In our neighborhood, residents were being robbed by criminals posing as service workers. So doom felt very, very close. In my anxious state, I spent hours in my own home planning and visualizing how I would kill an intruder by throwing stuffed animals at his head to distract him long enough to grab a paring knife to stab him in the eye socket. Then I would tie him to a chair and make him watch *Baby Einstein* and *Teletubbies* so in his last moments on earth he would feel totally nutty. Like me. At least someone would then finally know my pain.

But unlike me, at least the intruder I killed would get to have a good night's sleep. I was too busy to sleep. We had about a month to sell our house, buy a house, procure a job for my husband, and find a new school for Lucy. We spent more days driving back and forth the three hours between San Francisco and Nevada City so that Rolf could go to job interviews. We'd park in the grocery store parking lot and he would change his clothes in the car with his butt hanging out the window, but we didn't have anywhere else to go.

Our Nevada County realtor was confused by our need-it-done-yesterday city slicker ways, but nonetheless, he showed us all the properties we'd downloaded from real estate websites the night before. We drove around and checked out all the possible schools Lucy might attend. The days ticked by. In San Francisco, the school year would be starting in two weeks. And we were still scrambling to get everything in place.

Looking back to that hectic, gut-wrenching time period, I guess it's not too surprising that Rolf's appendix would burst.

Ugh. Who had time to drop everything and have surgery? It's possible that yes, he could have died, but that little extended vacay in the emergency room was highly inconvenient. I remember him lying on the gurney as I put a pen in his hand to sign papers like he was a dying octogenarian and I was Anna Nicole Smith. I remember thinking, *Don't die now, baby; we're in the middle of escrow!* Rolf doesn't remember much from his hospital stay. As my mom, who is prone to malapropisms, would say, "It was all just a blurb."

After more lost sleep, and one fewer organ later, it was time to bust a move. Something inside me had snapped. We had to leave. I felt so beholden to an enormous, abstract responsibility in my hometown—to family members, to frenemies, to Chinese neighbors who expected me to talk or act differently. Strangers appeared hostile, and every corner of the city seemed overcrowded and outlandishly expensive. Affording an education for Lucy seemed out of reach, and we were already treading water in debt.

I was ready to jettison our escape pod. Of course, the financials for a home loan took longer to come through than we expected. Rolf couldn't give notice at his San Francisco job because we wouldn't be able to get a loan if he was unemployed or even just newly employed. And we were in a pickle because we really didn't have any money to buy a new house until we sold the old house, and that hadn't happened yet. Our Bay Area, Asian American mortgage broker was working overtime for us, and in his good-natured exasperation he said to me, "Why are you moving to the middle of nowhere? Aren't there, like, no Asians up there? What are you going to do, open up a Panda Express?"

Oh, you're hilarious, Ted.

"For your information, they already have a Panda Express, thank you very much."

The only way to break out of the locked Chinese box was to leave San Francisco. I truly believed that there wasn't any room for a "new" kind of me to grow in my hometown. My world had shrunk, or I had painted myself into a corner. Any way you wanted to say it, I was stuck in the mud, and whichever way I tried to maneuver, I just sank deeper.

Sometimes you have to break down a door with all your might. What remains of the crash is a splintered, bloody mess. But at least you're still alive and kickin'. And that's how I felt then. Like I had to leave to stay alive.

So screw me and the Subaru I rode out on. Life in San Francisco ended with a creaking sound. An aching, wet, wooden pier down at the wharf, or maybe China Basin, was groaning. A ship was moored beside it, and the planks pulled against the weight of the vessel as it tried to accelerate away. *SNAP! SNAP! SNAP!* The ropes were giving way, breaking, whipping up as they did. The wooden pier felt its xylophone skeleton being pulled apart, then fell back into a slump, causing a small but significant tidal wave.

The boat that got away was being paddled by human hands. Ours. Mine. We were away. The skyline receded, and the familiar red neon letters faded away, the ones that spelled out PORT OF SAN FRANCISCO. We floated away on the Bay, and then under the Golden Gate Bridge to the open waters of the Pacific. The gentle lapping of the ocean and our breathing, our panting from exhaustion, were the only noises, and seagulls.

We risked everything to leave.

And oh, the creaking. I still hear it in my dreams, and in

my waking life, too. I detect the faint sounds of the moaning wooden pier as the tide rushes in and out. The moorings did not hold. I loosened the bonds myself and threw my body against the feeling of something constricting me. Before I knew it, restraints that I imagined were made of silk finally snapped. The braided strands had never been even a little bit frayed, but the next moment I found myself on the floor, broken free. Free to go.

As the song goes, "San Francisco, here is your wanderin' one / Saying I'll wander no more." But I had never wandered, never strayed even once. I got up and left the only place I ever knew. My city. A lot of people belong to her and she to them, and they came from near and far. Sayonara.

And yet. And yet. Still I hear those plaintive cries, the moans and whispers. They say, "Come back. Come back. Please, daughter. Please, friend. Come back, honey."

And all night, in the brightest moonlight, it still keeps me awake, night after night in Nevada City.

As I write this right now, I've just had to stop and pause because Lucy is showing me her latest book, *The Mice Go On, Volume 26.* She has been working on these books that she has stapled together for about a year now, and this is the latest adventure. The series is about a mouse named Squeak and all the calamities from which he escapes. For instance, once a water bottle floods his mouse hole; another time a cat attacks him and his friends; and another time a mousetrap almost captures him in its clutches. The pages are filled with mishaps, foiled plans, and harebrained schemes that always end up working out just fine. No matter what chaos takes place, every volume of *The Mice Go On* concludes in the very same, satisfying way. It's very simple. The last page of every book is blank except for one sentence, "And everything was OK."

And so it was for us. We left San Francisco and moved to Nevada City. We found a new job for Rolf and a new school for Lucy. We lasted long enough in the city to not get flattened in the crosswalk or disfigured by a deranged bull mastiff. We were pretty wobbly at first, but like a mother mouse in one of my daughter's homemade books, I just kept telling myself that everything would be okay.

22

Aeon Flux Capacitor

Even after I left my hometown, or maybe because of this drastic change, I remained fascinated with the life trajectories of Asian Americans who don't want to follow the routes their parents delineate for them. Some have gone ahead and gotten that medical degree or passed the bar exam, but they know in their hearts that they don't want to practice medicine or law. Others of us have followed the path of our dreams even though our parents have warned us that it only leads to the poorhouse. I suppose we are all struggling to escape what is expected of us.

I think of Yoda saying to Luke Skywalker, "Luminous beings are we," and that reminds me of the fluidity of ideas and feelings, and of how we don't have to pigeonhole ourselves, even though we might consider our bodies and personalities as already set in stone.

We can be a lot of things and feel a lot of ways. But who says we can't change if we want to? One day we can be more generous than usual, or less hidden, or less controlling, and more accepting. I think there are unexplored parts of every person's heart. Let's go spelunking.

To want another life other than the one you currently have can be an elusive pursuit. You can't capture it under glass, this mysterious thing that moves in and around us, hiding and revealing itself to us in its own sweet time. Our ambitions and desires for change are constantly in alternating modes, either stirring us into a frenzy or half hibernating in the dark. Our ambition is alive in a cave, in the sunlight, in the air. While we go about our business, this unknowable thing skips around. We feel weak from it sometimes, to have a sense of it flitting around—from me, to you, to other people we see on the street, or through everybody, within anybody else filled with a desperate desire for "something else."

Being a Chinese American today is to have your spirit in a stream, with those glimmering, shimmering particles too infinitesimal to scoop out, like gold flecks in river water. An American in a Chinese body is always panning for gold. You become part of the water, or else the gold becomes part of you as you cup your hands together and bring a drink of that rushing water to your lips. No matter if you speak English, Cantonese, or Mandarin, there's always a sweetness on the tongue, but also a thirst that can't be quenched.

In life, the not-knowing of never trying is worse than the knowing of doing and failing. As you try different ways of being, and eliminate what doesn't work for you, your desires are constantly changing shape, like water. Your aspirations can drip maddeningly off the storm drain or wash clean a window so you can see better. Sometimes water floods, or merely moistens, or can carry you back or forward like a tidal wash, or might crash down and bring destruction like a wave at Mavericks. As we swim with or against the currents, we go in and out like specks. Water can wash, or it can drown.

You might have a sensation that there's somewhere else you're supposed to be. In New York, Shanghai, San Francisco, Beijing, Hong Kong, or Los Angeles, your body in space, whether you are surrounded by many other Asians or if you are the only one around for miles, you feel a heat that doesn't burn, like a slow pouring of liquid on your skin. It doesn't stain, but can penetrate and coat you invisibly, like a protection or salve. There is always a yearning that time cannot wrestle to the ground.

Sometimes what we want or think we want feels like a barren branch, but slowly, like right before a rain, plump little birds come and perch one by one. And then there are those tiny birds that travel in clouds, and they can look like a swarm of bees from a distance.

Speaking of which, three days before we moved from San Francisco, my husband was standing on a ladder. He was painting the outside trim of the windows of our old house, and he turned around when he heard a low, humming noise. He didn't see anything at first, as it took a moment for his brain to make sense of what his eyes were looking at. A section of the sky was vibrating, moving like a dim, shivering spotlight. A thick, buzzing noise became louder. It was an electric sound.

It was a swarm of bees headed right for him. He was standing on the highest rung of a twelve-foot ladder with nowhere to go. Right before the swarm might have enveloped him, it careened to the left and crashed into the windows of the house next door. He climbed down and stood in the driveway catching his breath.

Later that day we were telling this story to a passerby who casually commented, "That's what happens when the old hive gets too crowded. The queen leaves to find a new home."

"What happens to the old hive?"

"Before she goes, the queen leaves behind eggs that will become new queens. She takes half the hive with her to the new home, and the other half stays. The swarm splits in two."

I thought about the bee incident and this conversation. Our hive had gotten too crowded with others' needs and wants that displaced our own. We were overburdened with our families' expectations and dependencies. Newcomers could and would always build their hives in San Francisco, and I had left to make room for them, and to make room for myself somewhere else, too. I didn't need to worry about my old town being taken care of. There would always be new artists, new inhabitants, and native sons and daughters born every day. I could go find a new home.

Two days later, I was collecting the last remnants of our belongings in the house and giving the floor a final sweep. I heard a familiar squawking noise, but it was a cacophony that seemed out of place. It was a North Beach sound out in the Sunset District. I shuffled to the window and looked up. Perched there on the electrical wire directly in front of me were the wild parrots of Telegraph Hill. For my whole life I had never once seen them this far west in the city. And there they were, those cheery green conures with the red heads and bright white circles around their eyes. Maybe it wasn't the whole flock, but thirty or so parrots were balancing on the wire, flipping like trapeze artists, and shouting out a hello, or a good-bye.

I watched them for a long time, their bird antics both charming and saddening me. "What are you doing out here, fellas?" I asked them out loud. They squawked and squeaked as I watched them play and fight, groom and preen. I didn't know how they found me, or why I felt the need to pretend their flight and visit had anything to do with me personally. When they suddenly and abruptly flew off in a haphazard tussle through the air, they were so clumsy and comical that I laughed out loud.

"Bye, guys," I said, watching their bright green bodies blend like a group of dots into the blue of the sky until they were gone. Rather, they blended so effortlessly into the background that I thought they were gone, but they were still there, of course, just continuing their adventures elsewhere, less sentimental than this San Franciscan.

I had been living in San Francisco with a husband, home, and new baby. Both sides of my Chinese family had a C-clamp on my soul, and the stress of city living was squeezing an ever-tightening grip around my shoulders. My nerves were frayed like electrical lines that had been blown down in a thunderstorm, live and exposed, ready to ignite at the slightest provocation.

I felt the gathering storm clouds although I could not see them. I was sure that something bad could be just around the corner. Was it just paranoia? Perhaps. But I didn't want to find out the hard way.

Each day I feared that I might get squished in the street. Even if I was between the two painted lines of the crosswalk, I could very likely become Pedestrian #17 to get annihilated that year in the Cool, Grey City of Love. A truck could flatten me or a cyclist might knock me over as it flew through a red light. Perhaps I would never seen it coming.

Maybe I felt so vulnerable because my C-section had changed me. After all, my body had been taken apart and put back together again, and in the process a new human was born. My hometown suddenly felt menacing to me. I was overwhelmed with an impending sense of doom, as if everything that had once felt assuring and familiar could now potentially kill me.

And like that swarm of bees, I felt split in two.

One morning I woke up in Nevada City and looked out the window to find snow melting in the sunlight. It took a while for my pupils to adjust. After my warm slumber behind dark curtains, I was temporarily blinded by the sun-slicked leaves of the trees outside. Droplets of clear slush dripped from the branches like crystals hanging from a chandelier. The night sky had burned away. I continued to watch the melting snow slide from the trees to the ground in slow-motion free fall, half between snowflakes and rain. Steam was rising everywhere, and the natural world transformed right before my eyes.

Where else was frost melting? Somewhere inside me.

Caught between two worlds, we are all in our own version of the Middle Kingdom. There's who we're expected to be, who we'd like to be, and where we live, the in-between. We all inhabit that secret cave where we've been spelunking. Beneath the rocks, the cave opens up to a spacious wellspring where fresh water gurgles up, and the sunlight from above reflects and glimmers, casting wavy light into the shadows.

Asian Americans, we hide ourselves too well. No one is going to crawl under a rock to get us. We have to come out into the light.

PART 4

Emerging from the Shadows
and into the Light

23

Trying to Calm the Inner Hysteria

What kind of idiot *leaves* San Francisco? I left my house, my family, my city of riveting, bright ocean light and foggy, romantic skies. I knew all the shortcuts in SF, the one-way alleys, secret parking spots, and clean bathrooms downtown. I knew which magnolia tree bloomed earliest in Golden Gate Park and could identify the sandy stretch of beach where the plentiful, perfect, unbroken sand dollars washed up after a storm.

How could I leave that complicated nest, my place of knowledge, my beating heart where the blood rushed through my veins, thumping loudly like the Pacific Ocean crashing against Seal Rock?

I immediately missed walking by the Flood Building that used to be Woolworth's that used to be the Baldwin Hotel. I longed to eat a cheeseburger in a dark-paneled room with Maxfield Parrish's *Pied Piper* glowing golden on the wall behind glass and crystal decanters. I wanted to touch my fingertips to the red velvet and silver wallpaper at C. Bobby's Owl Tree.

The memories and ghosts I thought I was fleeing instead just took up residence in a kaleidoscopic corner of my brain, and I still could see the faraway images like from a coin-slotted pay telescope at Playland-at-the-Beach. I could place a dime in the slot on the side of my head and here's what would unfurl:

My brother's wedding at the Empress of China, afterward sitting in the Palace Hotel's Garden Court in an inky-black gown, my husband in a tuxedo and my baby daughter still just a twinkle in her daddy's eye. And Café Europa on Columbus Avenue, El Tapatio on Francisco Street, the old U.S. Restaurant, Pronto Pup, Uncle's Café, Joe Jung's, and everywhere snacks, pastries, chow fun, ice cream, and those fancy Parisian macaroons that, for two, cost more than I was paid per hour at my first job at Pier 39.

San Francisco was where my mom worked in a curio shop as a kid in Chinatown, where my grandparents raised seven kids and ran a travel agency. It's where my dad's father died at Kaiser in 1962 the day he was supposed to go home after a routine operation. My dad worked in the Transamerica Pyramid, that pointed dunce cap on the paper cutout skyline, and we all went to school, worked, had piano lessons, Chinese school, and basketball practice while joyous and tragic things happened all around us, like one moment going to the Ice Follies at Winterland, and then getting a phone call and finding out that a friend's dad was stabbed to death on Van Ness Avenue by a guy who'd just robbed the Crocker Bank.

That was my city, or just a twenty-second silent film of it. A snapshot, really. But, hey, I'm not the only one to feel longing and love and pride in San Francisco. I'm the one who left, after all. But all those images are what roll around in your head, everyone's head, I suppose, all in a jumble when you're from a place.

Now that I'd left my hometown, had it left me? I refrained from buying a SAN FRANCISCO sweatshirt and wearing it around my new town. That would've drawn exactly the kind of attention I didn't want. My heartbroken mopiness was already a big scab on my face. Wearing a hoodie with an SF logo would have been advertising the ache that still woke me in the night.

What had I done? In the following months, I opened many bottles of champagne and assured myself it would be okay. I baked dozens of chocolate chip cookies, cheesecakes, and blueberry pies to keep my hands from shaking. I told myself that a lot of formidable people had loved both my old town and my new town: Lotta Crabtree, Lola Montez, and all those old-timey writers we all claim to love but have never actually read. Nevada City is as old as San Francisco, with similar sights and sounds of bygone rowdiness. In my head I saw the gold bullion, the veins of silver in the mines, the gilt wallpaper, and murdered Chinamen.

I left so I could find out something new about myself, to see what lay beyond my childhood playground.

However. There was nowhere to hide now. There was no ocean air to soothe me, no fog to enshroud me. I looked for the old familiar sights—snowy plovers, bottlebrush trees, eucalyptus, and miles of concrete sidewalk. But now there would be no grid to follow, no straight shot up Market Street, no waterfront or end of the earth scattered with broken bits of shells and nineteenth-century brick. I touched my hand to the ground and searched unsuccessfully. Now all I felt was new dirt beneath my flip-flops, with not even one jewel of green sea glass to remind me of what came before. Unmoored and unprotected, I might've stayed safe if I had remained in San Francisco. She would've watched over me, my city. She would've made sure I didn't do anything stupid.

And by leaving San Francisco, I figuratively and literally left my mother.

Mom, bring me a Popsicle kept cold by fog, a glass of milk frosted with Ocean Beach air. Out there the orange crabs are Dungeness, but the basement crawl spaces crammed with my childhood memories were *dungeon-esque*. But now, I had sold off my baggage and all my treasures. I gave them up for a few dollars at the Alemany Flea Market, and the rest of my stuff I dragged to the corner of Twenty-Second Avenue and Ortega where, in mere minutes, San Franciscans who'd chosen to stay stopped their cars and picked clean my former belongings—CP Shades cotton culottes, Fisher-Price wooden people, *Star Wars* action figures, and satin pillows with Chinese brocade.

At the garage sales, in Cantonese, Russian, and English, my neighbors wouldn't buy these collected bits of my life for twenty-five cents, but the siren song of the word *FREE* written in black Sharpie, combined with a latitude and longitude posted on Craigslist, whisked away all my mementos in seconds flat.

San Francisco. You and I had begun our trial separation. After about a year, I still missed you. The smell of your hair (which is the salt air) and the feel of your caress across my face on a cold day were elements I still longed for. I remembered when you'd reach for me, but instead, I'd thrust my hands in my pockets, believing I didn't need your touch.

Back then, at least you knew I was probably just walking to one of your libraries, like a little kid pretending I was running away from home but just going to a neighbor's house. San Francisco, Mother, Mom, you always knew where to find me—at the public library or in Golden Gate Park. You had memorized all my favorite hiding places. You knew I was always somewhere within reach, walking on your downtown sidewalks or warming myself in a well-lit place with books, either in a ticky-tacky house, an Edwardian apartment, or a store of nooks and crannies on Clement Street.

Did I make the right decision?

I hadn't realized I was in a locked Chinese box until, out of desperation, I tried the door and found it unlatched. The only way I found to flee the Chinese cage of expectation, family obligations, and guilt was to physically move away. I realized that I was an adult, and it was my responsibility to improve my circumstances if I wasn't happy.

The only way to change myself on the inside was to start on the outside. We moved out of San Francisco, and the jolt of that upheaval unshackled me from other people's constricting ideas of who I am. By moving, I did something no one expected I could or would ever do. Of course, I also inadvertently detonated my entire support system. There would be no more free babysitting from my parents, and no old friends to lean on if I ever felt insecure.

Leaving my clan and all my familial connections was a very un-Chinese thing to do.

But then again, it was a very Chinese American thing to do. All the early Chinese immigrants to San Francisco left their families and customs behind and started fresh in a new land. We are all the descendants of those who embarked on adventures toward new continents and new identities. And let's face it, I didn't travel across an ocean, but just three hours away by car.

San Francisco and my mother loved me enough to let me fly away. Maybe they knew I'd instinctively behave like some kind of homing pigeon, with a scrap of paper, a note of hopeful optimism, tied to my leg.

Maybe they knew it would be impossible for me to stay away permanently. After all, for San Franciscans, the impulse to return is always strong. We've been trained through experiences, written instructions, and books we've reread so many times that we confuse city lore with our own memories. Like homing pigeons, city natives have been thrown from the rooftops so many times, but always remember how to come back. We go from downtown to Ocean Beach, and whichever direction we fly, we look to the horizon, to the skyline, and to the corners of buildings, and we reorient ourselves back to the place we love.

Both San Francisco and my mother take me back every time. Yeah, they take me back. Like they've been waiting for me with the porch light on. Like dinner's been warming on the stove and both city and mother have just been reading in a chair, pretending they're not staying awake for any particular reason. Just up all night, San Francisco. It's the city that knows how . . . to feign sleep.

If the side door isn't open, I look for the key hidden under the rock. It's never under the doormat because there are hardly any doormats in San Francisco. They keep getting stolen off the front stoop. But that doesn't matter. The absence of doormats doesn't mean that I or anyone else is any less welcome.

Approaching San Francisco from either the Bay or Golden Gate Bridge, with the mesh blanket of quiet city lights, it sometimes looks like no people inhabit the streets at all. The grid of lit-up squares and rectangles is actually a myriad of individual apartments and houses, and as I get closer, I hope to see that one window that is my window. When I'm lost and can't figure out which is mine, like *Harold and the Purple Crayon,* I draw my family home where I want it to be.

When I arrive, I imagine that both the city and my mother see me standing there. They just look at my face, whether I've got my hands in my pockets or my arms are loaded with luggage. Sometimes I've got my backpack, or else I might have a suitcase with a broken strap and that elastic rainbow thing holding it together.

San Francisco, you don't even ask me any questions. Like I said, you just look at my face. I don't know if it's dirty or if my lipstick is smeared; you just look at me for a long moment before you say, and it's always the same thing, "Well, you might as well come inside and have something to eat."

And likewise, my mom doesn't hug me. Nor does she look disappointed, or say shame on you or I told you so. When I go to the back room, I see the bed is made, but it's not done up for a guest. It's my bed, but the sheets and blankets are slightly mussed like someone's been lying down, not inside but just atop the coverlet. That slight depression on my bed is how I know someone has been waiting up. When I lay my body down and place my face gently against the pillowcase, San Francisco, it smells like you.

24

Flap Your Wings

When we left San Francisco, my parents were not exactly happy for me. Actually, they were probably completely bereft. I was their baby. I was their only girl, and in the unspoken ways of Chinese culture, I was supposed to be the one who stayed behind to take care of them. Who, in the years to come, would change their adult diapers and make sure they weren't surviving on tins of Fancy Feast? They were still completely able-bodied and sharp-minded, but the idea that the daughter they'd raised would suddenly pack up and take off must have felt like a real slap in the face.

And as if that wasn't enough of an insult, I'd also taken away not just their albino workhorse, but beautiful Baby Lucy, too. At the time we left, Lucy had just turned five years old and was the apple of their eyes. She was happy and silly and made them young in a way none of us had anticipated. Caring for her gave them a second chance as "parents" to do all the things they had been too busy to do with my brothers and me. As doting grandparents they took Lucy to the pumpkin patch, to the beach, and on Disneyland vacations. They spoiled her with trips to Dairy Queen and bought her stuffed animals I would've killed for when I was a kid.

All of which came to an abrupt end when I pulled up our stakes and set our dinghy upon uncharted waters. I can't remember if my parents decided officially to not speak to me, or if I was just too busy and wrecked myself to notice that I had caused them intense grief.

And in my defense, all I can say is that I knew they were mad. And I knew they were sad. But how could I explain that I did the only thing I could to stay alive? I was completely and honestly just that desperate.

Someone asked me if I had moved away to "get back" at my mother. At the time, my immediate reaction was, "What are you talking about?" In retrospect, perhaps it is plausible to see things that way, but that had never been my motivation.

I was the one hurting inside, and I was the one feeling crushed, although I wasn't quite aware then of how my family was part of that equation. Sometimes you just have to knock yourself out of a bad groove. Then later, you can go back and pick up the pieces, or ruminate for years about why you did what you did.

I felt selfish, but maybe selfish is good sometimes. Maybe if Iris Chang had been less selfless, she'd still be around. Although it sounds callous, at times I really did imagine saying to my parents, "Just be glad I didn't escape by driving off a cliff. In comparison, living three hours away doesn't sound so bad, does it?"

Months went by, and during that time my parents and I had

the occasional, terse phone conversation. I was busy trying to get my sea legs in our new town and helping Lucy adjust to her new school. Rolf was getting acclimated to his new job, and we were still unpacking everything, unsure of our new lives.

The truth is that I have no idea what was going through my Tiger Mom's mind or heart when I up and left home. Was she angry and fixated on how I'd done her wrong, or were her thoughts tinged with her own regrets? Did she miss me, or just miss knowing I was there because micromanaging me gave her something to do?

Above all else, I am sure she truly missed Lucy. But what could I do?

When you're on an airplane, during the instructions for an emergency landing, they always say to put on your own air mask before assisting others. You have to secure your own safety before you can help others to survive. And breaking free was securing my own oxygen supply.

I didn't leave San Francisco and take my daughter away from my mother to "get back" at her. A baby bird grows up and eventually leaves the nest. It was simply time for me to spread my wings, and fly away.

25

Who's Biting Your Style?

The new home we found was half a block away from the school where Lucy would start kindergarten. The school was a quaint, WPA-built structure complete with a bell at the top and students inside singing "America the Beautiful."

I was aware that if Lucy had gone to a San Francisco public school, she probably would have been one of the least Chinese-looking kids in her class with her brown hair and mixed facial features. I had been planning on having to navigate the waters of my child being seen as not Chinese enough. But here, having popped my head into Lucy's kindergarten class at Nevada City Elementary, I was surprised to see that my daughter would not only be the sole nonwhite student in her class, but she was practically the only *brunette*. A few minutes later I was mulling over this irony in the school office while I filled out some papers for the secretary. I handed her my forms and she looked closely at my address and broke into a huge smile.

"Oh, you will be so glad you moved here," she said with obvious delight. "Lucy will have so much fun playing with the white kids!"

Uh . . . what?

No doubt my race hackles were always on alert, but really. REALLY? I stood wide-eyed and mute for a full twenty seconds.

The secretary then went on to explain that she knew my neighbors, the Whites, whose two school-age daughters were also enrolled at the school. I breathed a sigh of relief.

"Oh," I said. "The Whites. I get it!"

I must admit, though, it was pretty weird going from the city, where thinking about different ethnicities was always somewhat in my mind, to a small town, where racial homogeneity was the norm. There were a few nonwhites here and there, but for the most part, it didn't look too diverse from the outside. There were all different sorts of *white* people—retirees and families, conservatives and liberals, rich homeowners and homeless guys loitering around downtown. There was also a contingent of alternative lifestylers in a big vegetarian, pot-growing, blond-with-dreadlocks kinda scene. So yes, there was indeed a lot of variety in the all-white population, like going to a paint store and finding everything from cream to titanium, blanc de chine, alabaster, and antique white. But nonvanilla flavors were generally not too well represented here.

This apparent lack of diversity was especially surprising because Nevada City did once have a sizable Chinese population. Here at the foot of the Sierras, Nevada City was once known as the Queen of the Northern Mines, and it was a thriving community that sprang up after the discovery of gold in

1848 in Coloma near Sacramento. In the late 1800s, Nevada City was California's third-largest city after San Francisco and Sacramento. Here and in the surrounding areas, hundreds of Chinese men came seeking fortune. They found work, but they also encountered discrimination, poor treatment, and outright attacks.

The Chinese were affected also by legislation that debilitated them at every turn—a foreign miners' tax aimed specifically at them, the Chinese Exclusion Act limiting immigration from 1882 until its repeal in the 1940s, laws forbidding marriage between races, regional taxes on wearing the Chinese hairstyle (the queue), and even taxes and legislation against carrying baskets on poles. Additionally, Chinese workers were allocated only the areas of land considered to be already stripped of gold, or fishing and shrimping areas that were believed to be depleted.

The thrifty and tenacious Chinese, however, often did more with fewer resources. They swallowed their pride to take jobs that other workers would not deign to do. Also, they banded together for protection. Their strength in numbers and ability to survive in varied conditions were perceived by other ethnic groups as threatening. From San Francisco to Sacramento, and from Nevada City to other mining towns and rural areas in between, the Chinese population that achieved so much for the railroads, gold mines, and infrastructure for the West often was rewarded with only derision, physical violence, and murder.

I think often of this local history as I walk the streets of Nevada City now, more than one hundred years later. I am frequently the only Asian face I see all day, maybe even all week, save for my own daughter's. Occasionally I do see some Japanese Americans around, the surrounding area having once been home to Japanese fruit growers, but after the internment of Japanese Americans in World War II, their numbers had also diminished drastically. The descendants of the original Chinese miners have mostly all moved on to bigger cities with more opportunities. I have not yet once met a single Chinese person here whose family came and stayed throughout the changing economic times.

So what of them is left here? I live one block from the old Chinese part of town, and nearby is a plaque and a memorial fountain where vagrants hang out in the native grasses, smoking nonnative weed. The remaining buildings that were once occupied by an opium den, a laundry, a couple of shops, and a residence are now remodeled structures that house a Thai restaurant, a trinket shop, and a couple of boutiques. The stores sell sculptures of Buddhas and accentuate an Asian vibe with meditation books and paraphernalia, candles, lotions, incense, and mandala carvings. It's all pretty blissed out, and sometimes, in the corner of the window displays are old photos of Chinese residents or opium smokers to both show what came before and to infuse the businesses with the romance of Orientalism.

When we first arrived here we attended an idyllic, small-town Constitution Day parade, which is held every year, ostensibly to celebrate the signing of the U.S. Constitution. A nearly identical parade occurs each Mardi Gras and every other Fourth of July. The kids love it, and it is indeed fun for the whole family, and for all the town's residents. So far, in the four years we've lived here, we've attended this main street attraction several times. Included in the festivities are middle school and high school marching bands, local businesses in a motorcade, Shriners in their tiny cars whizzing around in figure eights, and local service groups and unions strolling past and sometimes handing out candy, American flags, or plastic Mardi Gras beads.

Amid this parade of local color is also an anemic, three-person contingent carrying a Chinese drum and brass cymbals, knocking out a little tune barely reminiscent of the clanging, heart-pounding beats at the San Francisco Chinese New Year parade. I wasn't really expecting any Chinese representation at all, but frankly, I wonder if nothing would be better than this strange little something. Only one guy of the three is actually Asian, and the other two have embarrassing Fu Manchu mustaches and are dressed in flashy robes. I am so undone by this paltry salute to my heritage that I am still unsure if they actually represent an official group of any kind or exist as simply an offhanded hey-how-ya-doing from the ghosts of Chinamen past. Every time I spot this small group, I wonder how I might lure a real San Francisco or Sacramento kung fu school here for the next parade to do justice to the area's local Chinese history. But inertia being what it is, regrettably my wishful thinking dissipates as they amble past and the next attraction distracts me.

And if you want to know if I've ever experienced any discrimination here, the answer is no. If asked to speculate why, I'd have to point out that there are so few Asians in town that we pose no threat in numbers. The history of prejudice and antagonism against the Chinese had everything to do with quantity. Before so many Chinese immigrated to the United States, city and town residents throughout the West showed more tolerance of their presence, however begrudging. I once saw a photo of a Chinese vegetable garden from the 1800s that was smack-dab in what is now Pacific Heights in San Francisco. However, as time went on, and the public perceived that the immigrant "celestials" were coming in droves, the Chinese were confined to only certain areas of town, and newspaper cartoons began to depict Chinese people as rats pouring off the ships in unstoppable numbers.

As soon as a few strangers turn into many, their "otherness" becomes more apparent and, simultaneously, more abhorrent. Their strangeness cannot be absorbed or diluted by a majority, so a group once considered innocuous enough is then viewed as a potential threat. The same trend occurred in mining areas as well. A handful of Chinese in the camps was one thing, but once there were more than could be counted, their foreign customs added to the overall rancor among miners who were all competing for the scant gold that was getting harder and harder to find. This dynamic set off a domino effect of discrimination and abuse. It is apparent even today in modern suburban communities when urban Chinese move to surrounding areas and form new shopping areas or pockets of residences. Even if Asians are the only group moving in to revitalize an area, it isn't long before they are targeted for derision even if it was solely their gumption and sweat equity that made the old, run-down sections of town safe, lively, or even vaguely palatable and therefore valuable to the local real estate market and businesses.

But now in Nevada City, despite the history of abuse toward Chinese in the past, there are definitely not enough of us here to pose any kind of imposition to the greater whole. We are in no danger of developing into a majority; rather, we are easily diluted into the creamy hue of eggshell white. I have always felt accepted and welcomed here and have known no hostility from my fellow townspeople. If more Asians or Asian Americans did happen to move to the area, who knows what might ensue.

Perhaps when faced with the onslaught of more numerous or less-Americanized strangers, folks might offer me olive branch statements such as "But you're different," or "You're not like them," or "You're white anyway." In college, none of these statements ever actually reassured me the way they were intended. Thus, even those of us who are fully Americanized are still subjected, however infrequently, to these occasional, qualifying statements. And we always recognize that slow, sinking feeling, that knowledge that in other people's eyes, we are always intrinsically different.

If you don't really get what I'm talking about, think back to that movie *Pretty Woman*. It's just like when Richard Gere says to Julia Roberts, "I've never treated you like a prostitute." When he walks away, she gets teary, as if she can't believe he just said that. Then she says to herself, "You just did." That's what I'm talkin' about. Even if a Chinese American's thoughts of racial difference are temporarily not in the forefront of her thoughts, anyone—a stranger, a friend, or a mogul you've recently fellated in the penthouse of a five-star hotel—might at any time unleash an unexpected bon mot to bring home the reality that your race always means something to somebody.

But back to downtown Nevada City.

I remember the first time we ate at the Chinese restaurant on Broad Street. The owner came to our table and asked, "What are you doing here? Visiting from out of town?"

This was not the first time that a proprietor of a Chinese restaurant had come out from the kitchen to inquire about where we'd come from or why we were there. It happened several times when Rolf and I traveled the Southwest, years before we had Lucy. Here in California, though, I hadn't thought a Chinese face would be so unique.

"We just moved from San Francisco," I said. "We live two blocks away now."

The Chinese man grimaced and looked at us in disbelief. He said, "Why would anyone *leave* San Francisco?"

Rolf and I looked at each other. It was our first week here and we were still reeling from our whirlwind move, wondering indeed if we had made a mistake. Rolf said, "Um, I'm feeling a little fragile about that right now. Could we not talk about that and just order our food?"

For the first weeks, months, and year, we walked through town and tried to get the feel of the place. Nevada City's old buildings compose the most comprehensive group of existing Gold Rush–era structures in the West. Within the population, there are families who have been here for many generations. But who knows? Maybe you're not considered a local until you've lived here for twenty years. The checkers at the grocery store only really started talking to me after we'd lived here for three years. I have never before lived in a small town so I have always been aware to mind my p's and q's. I didn't want to come here and declare anything about myself. I wanted to see what might come to me on its own. And so it was with the Chinese thing, too. I wanted to absorb whatever I found here, and not step on anyone's toes. But, hey, I do have to leave the confines of my house sometimes, and when you walk among the people, toes do get accidentally stepped on.

There's a guy who runs a fancy Chinese trinket shop in town. At first I thought it was a little odd that he's never been very friendly to me. I can't tell if he's just cranky, or if he's being vigilant because he thinks my kid is going to knock something over. We are always very careful and respectful when we enter his shop, which is filled to the brim with Asian knickknacks like Quan Yin statuettes, fancy teapots, silk pillows, feng shui handbooks, and various doodads adorned with the faces and lithe figures of Asian ladies. The owner's eyes follow me each time I'm there, as if he fears I'm gonna shoplift something really expensive. You'd think that I'd be that store's target audience, its ultimate consumer, but no. He scowls at me like I'm some toothless meth addict asking to use his bathroom.

And similarly, there's a scholarly gentleman who runs the local museum with Chinese artifacts. He wants no part of me either. We toured the historic building where he educates visitors cheerfully, and after talking with him, I did send him a couple of e-mails on topics he seemed interested in. I was appropriately respectful of his knowledge and his position. But there was no love connection there either. I initially thought he'd be delighted to talk to someone who was familiar with the Chinese Historical Society in San Francisco and other organizations he mentioned. However, any time I seemed a little too informed about the Square and Circle Club (a service organization of Chinese women that my mother once belonged to), or a Chinese American artist, or the famous photos of Chinatown by Arnold Genthe, he just got more irritable. I guess he was the one used to doing the teaching, and he was a little peeved that I wasn't a completely unformed vessel.

So I've been thinking about these two gents for some time now. Maybe there can only be a couple of scholars on Asian culture around here, and these two guys have already divvied up the territory. They both deal in a certain romanticism about the area's Chinese history. The museum shows enlarged photos of Chinese residents from the late 1800s wearing silk finery, elaborate hairstyles, and old-fashioned shoes. The foreign charm and exotic details are very attractive. Likewise, the trinket shop wholly commodifies the Chinese past with decorations that play up the allure of Asian calm. In both cases, I am being sold a bill of goods here, except ironically, *I am the goods.*

To borrow a line from the movie *Swingers*, I guess we Asian Americans are "so money we don't even know how money we are." Chinese culture and what our faces represent apparently bring in the big bucks. But I'm not exactly sure how I feel about Asian-themed objects being so popular. I am conflicted. As a Chinese person, I feel objectified and a little embarrassed when I see a placemat or a coffee mug decorated with the winking face of an Asian woman. However, simultaneously, my American side might be attracted to the innocent romance of a 1930s Shanghai girl in a pretty cheongsam. It's definitely weird to see something for sale that has a picture on it that is not me per se, but simultaneously represents me. In stores, I never see shirts or stationery whose sole decoration is the face of a random white person, or any other race for that matter. In contrast, I was in a boutique with Lucy and she tugged on my sleeve with honest confusion and asked, "Why does that apron have a picture of Auntie Angie on it?" We both stared in disbelief because the silk-screened image did, in fact, bear an uncanny resemblance to my sister-in-law. "I don't know" was all I managed to say.

And thus, when you are Chinese American, even shopping is complicated.

Whether I am at the trinket shop or the museum, both of which seem to share the purpose of bringing Chinese culture to the public, there doesn't seem to be any room for a real Chinese person who can dispel the romanticism and mystique. In the selling of Oriental illusion, is my very presence a fly in the soy milk?

I'm not yet ready to make any further waves, so for now I'll just stay out of that particular store as well as that gallery of artifacts. I understand why I might make those men feel uncomfortable. Clearly, they think I am biting their style.

But fellow citizens, really. Dare we ask, who bit whose style first?

26

Welcome to What I Didn't Know

One thing nobody tells you about motherhood is that you will be surrounded all the time. Someone is always touching you, talking to you, grabbing at your clothes, or otherwise obliterating your personal space. Your hands are always busy making something, rearranging and fixing an object or favorite item, or cleaning clothes, toys, or household items. And while you are trying to apply laserlike focus to the tasks at hand, your child or spouse is grabbing at your rump or sundry lady parts, and you just want to tell everyone to please, please, just stop. Please. Just. Stop. Touching. Me.

Everyone is supposedly being playful and just wanting to be lovey-dovey, but how can you think about hot glue guns, Twizzlers, soccer cleats, feeling feminine, the overdue property tax, sex, camping gear for the overnight field trip, and making a stuffed angel hedgehog with wings out of napkins all at the same time?

And then you have to feel guilty for being crabby. And even feeling guilty feels like just one more thing you gotta do. Of course, meanwhile, you aren't even looking after your own basic needs, and you might suddenly notice that for the past hour you have been starving. I often discover that my stomach is rumbling, and I recall that before I had a kid, I used to frequently eat hot meals. Now I vaguely remember what those tasted like. Remember the mom in *A Christmas Story*? In the voice-over, Ralphie says, "My mother had not had a hot meal for herself in fifteen years." I always chuckled a little at that line until I became that line. For many years now I've made my daughter's dinner, then served the adult meal for my husband and me, but by the time I'm about to sit down, someone needs milk or water, and since I'm already the one who isn't eating yet, I am the one who ends up getting the drink, and then a fork is dropped or a drink is spilled, and by the time I settle down to take my first bite, the kid is done eating and wants something else, or suddenly has to poop. As I'm chewing that first mouthful of food, it is somewhat less appetizing knowing that any second now, someone will be yelling, "I NEED TO BE WIPED!"

Lather. Rinse. Repeat. Every single meal, of every single day, for the past nine years.

And I wish I was joking. But all you other moms out there know that I am not. As I ruminate on this daily situation, I have come to the realization that what I really want to say to my own mother is, "Sorry. I had no idea that this is what your life was like for *decades*."

Before I had my daughter I never realized I would never go

to the bathroom alone ever again. When she was a tiny infant, I used to strap her into the vibrating bouncy chair so she couldn't hurt herself while I was otherwise occupied for a couple of minutes. Later, when she was at the crawling stage, I locked the door with both of us inside so she couldn't scramble away and fall down the stairs. And from toddler age till now she has just wanted to be at my side at all times. It's wonderful that someone wants to accompany me for every bodily function I have, but it got old about seven years ago. Now she says, "Would you like some company?" which is really nice and polite, but frankly the answer is no.

I was reasonably prepared for the idea that an infant or toddler needs her mother to be physically close most of the time, but I am taken by surprise that the seven- to nine-year-old girl needs and wants her mom still, maybe even more. Kids want to sleep in a heap, like puppies. I want to sleep and not be kicked in the head. I would really appreciate some quiet any time of the day, but my kid likes to chatter constantly about kittens and mice and hamsters and which would I like better, a drawing of Russian or Chinese or Native American hedgehogs in Atlantis or an underground science fair where they grow magic blueberries that make them disappear and never grow old or die and always have chocolate caramel sundae parfaits for dinner and wear diapers that never smell bad?

She strings the sentences all together perhaps because she believes that as soon as she stops talking I will stop looking at her. That sounds logical. But here's the thing. She already gets tons of attention. She is an only child who lives with both her parents, and we are together all the time. And yet. Even for her, consistent attention is still not enough. When I see my daughter doing her version of "Egyptian tap dancing" complete with booty shakes and arm wiggling, I remember how desperately I also attempted to keep my own mother's gaze upon me. If she closed the door to go to the bathroom, it felt like the sun had suddenly been obscured by a dark cloud.

But enough already! Every mother I know has at one time or another waited hours to pee only to finally sit down and have a kid bang on the door like the house is on fire. When you waddle over to open the door with your pants still at your knees, it turns out the emergency is just that the kid couldn't peel a glitter sticker off its backing. So is it any wonder we want to drink wine all night?

And as the kid gets older, she is getting more and more curious about bodies. During the infant and toddler years, I took speed showers and barely spent time drying myself off or moisturizing. But I thought that after eight years I might get to take a somewhat normal shower. But no. I might be two days without bathing, and when I finally get in and feel the first three seconds of hot water awakening my skin, I think maybe I can finally relax for a minute. But then the curtain is yanked wide open for another urgent bit of news, "I CAN'T GET MY KINDLE TO WORK!" I am standing there naked as my daughter gapes at my body, wet boobs and all. Then my husband might stroll on in and say, "Ooh, what's going on in here?"

Please. Please, all of you. Please. Just. Get. Out.

When you are a mom, often it feels like the only time to yourself is when you are in the car. In your head, you hope that no one will want to go to the grocery store with you. You want to buy tampons in peace and not have to answer a barrage of questions like "Are those the thingies you stick in your butt?" or "Why do mommies have to wear diapers inside their underwear, anyway?"

Kids want to know everything. They want to touch, feel, and smell anything and everything about you. Some small person is always asking invasive questions about your deep, furrowed wrinkles ("Why do you have stripes on your forehead?"), your blubber ("That feels like pudding!"), or your breasts ("They kinda look like cupcakes, and that makes me hungry!").

Um, yeah.

So yes, Mom. I do apologize. I now know why you were so cranky. You were only as grumpy as I am now. We were all making you insane and I hadn't realized that mothers are like Rodney Dangerfield. Mothers don't get any respect.

As I look back, I recall that my own mom also wanted to be left alone. When I was younger, I couldn't imagine why she didn't want us crawling all over her with sticky hands, grabbing her face, and stepping all over her feet with our hard shoes. Our flailing limbs were constantly accidentally bonking her in the eyeball, side of the head, and anywhere else within our reach.

Ugh. Sorry, Mom. My bad. I get it now.

27

Dragon Lady Versus Pearl Concubine

I never applied for membership to the Hot Mess Club, but one day I suddenly realized I belonged. Somehow I already knew the exclusive address, and surprisingly, there was a reserved parking space right out front, just for me. Seemingly overnight there was a heap of crazy yelling from the kitchen and her name was Kim Wong Keltner.

I think every mother has asked herself at some point, *Why am I the one who has to do* everything? The quick answer is, because everyone has to do everything. What else is there to do, sit in the mush pot all day? For me, performing all the little tasks of every day is its own reward, a daily way of saying, "I'm grateful I have all my limbs."

It does feel exhausting sometimes though. However, I don't ever want to be like my friend Ann's mother. Every Sunday night she served a beautiful dinner that took all day to prepare, but when it came time to eat, she sat down at the table and sobbed uncontrollably into her hands. Meanwhile, the whole family ate in silence and pretended not to notice.

Ugh. For everybody. Note to self: Don't wanna cry at the dinner table no matter how exquisite the beef bourguignon.

When we first moved out of San Francisco, I was blown apart inside. Except for four years of college just over the bridge in Berkeley, I had never lived anywhere else but the city. If I was no longer a San Franciscan, I wasn't sure who or what to be. As a result, I defaulted to history's tried and true position for females, Nurturing Wife and Mother.

While my husband hit the ground running with his new job and my daughter began kindergarten, I made breakfast and careful lunches for them and had fresh-baked chocolate chip cookies waiting in the afternoon while dinner simmered on the stove. Since my daughter is sans siblings, frequently we hosted playdates, which also kept me busy preparing snacks and helping to set up elaborate stuffed animal tea parties and whatnot. I scurried around in a flowered apron with hot-pink trim, picking up toys and fetching glasses of milk.

As a kid I was always envious of the TV characters whose moms were home all day baking, ready with a hug and a pitcher of lemonade. And now I was that mom, and I found that the housewife role wasn't half bad.

For many months, in my delirium of having left my old life, I poured all my energy into being a good wife, a nurturing mother, and the fun mom to my daughter's little friends. Since I wasn't working a "regular" job, I had time to just enjoy the kids' company. In addition, we hosted big dinner parties where the parents came. Everyone played Ping-Pong and we stuffed our faces while our children enthusiastically turned the house upside down.

Week after week, month after month, I took it upon myself to take care of kids, prepare hors d'oeuvres, assemble lasagnas, bake brownies, mix salsas, and marinate veggies and meat for the barbecue. Every one of our friends is a hardworking, harried parent, and I was glad to offer snacks, relaxation, and a little pampering as if it was some higher calling.

I wanted to see how far I could push the servitude thing. I figured, hey, why do anything halfway? Chinese people are superior in everything, so I could be a better homemaker than even Carol Brady on TV. For me it was a novelty, and ironic, to behave in this way. Anyone who really knew me at all would know I wasn't a pushover or diminutive flower in any aspect of life, so this Asian-Female-at-Your-Service kind of thing was an interesting experiment.

Mind you, no one was asking me to act this way. No one was forcing me into this role. It just sort of began as a way to fill up time and not feel hysterical over having left everything I ever knew. But then again, I kept thinking of that Talking Heads song, and the lyrics, ". . . Well, how did I get here? Letting the days go by . . ."

And how *did* I get there? My meals got more and more elaborate. I was sweating eggplant and letting cheesecakes "breathe." And even though I knew I was acting nuts, I would blow a gasket if someone said they couldn't make it to dinner because they had a previous engagement. In my head, I sulked and thought, *How* dare *they not come over here and have the* most exquisite *time of their lives?!*

But then at some point, I remembered what Ann had told

me about her mother sobbing uncontrollably at the dinner table. *Oh, that's how that happens*, I realized. The martyr thing apparently just sneaks up on you. I didn't want to go to that wretched place, but I was making myself crazy trying to be a perfect wife and mom. No one forced me to strive for this ideal. I just started to automatically go there. If dinner and homemaking were something good, I could make them better. I could make things fantastic for everybody else, each and every day. I had fallen into the pursuit of perfection and didn't even know I was descending through a trapdoor that would leave me feeling ignored and, frankly, bored.

I had unknowingly, but most definitely, slipped over to a version of the Dark Side. Maybe it wasn't Tiger Mom Dark Side, but for sure it was Martha Stewart Dark Side, which was certainly related. It was the territory of Making Everything Right and to My Specifications, which should have at least made me suspicious. But instead, the persona of Control Freak was rather easy to slip into.

What now, genius?

I turned my thoughts to Chinese history. I remembered the story of Emperor Guangxu's sweet Pearl Concubine. I recalled the legend of how Empress Dowager Cixi, Guangxu's Tiger Mom, had the Pearl Concubine killed by ordering her to be thrown down a well. I asked myself if it mattered whether the Pearl Concubine was forcibly pushed to her death, or if she fell in by herself. Maybe she jumped in or was simply not paying attention and slipped carelessly. The reasons and the details of the Pearl Concubine's demise are lost to Qing Dynasty lore, but the end result is all we know: she perished.

I didn't want to lose myself in the classic feminine trap of endless people pleasing. I didn't realize how easy it was to absorb what society as a whole expected of a woman, to start acting accordingly, then to keep doing it because it did attract a certain amount of approval. I wanted to jab myself in the eye with a chopstick because I had turned into a maid. And worst of all, I had done it to myself.

Femininity and vulnerability are endlessly compelling and alluring. The legend of the Pearl Concubine was so fascinating because she represents the fantasy of the ultimate submissive Asian girl. There is a great painting by Zhong-Yang Huang of the Pearl being carried away by eunuchs. They are intent on throwing her down the well behind the Ningxi Palace in the Forbidden City. On the side of the painting, just out of full view, you can see Empress Dowager Cixi giving the execution order, and just below is the hand of her nephew, Emperor Guangxu, who is the Pearl Concubine's lover. She is his beloved and his only happiness in life, but as she desperately reaches for him, he does not save her. He was the emperor of China for heaven's sake. But he didn't do a damn thing to disobey history's most notorious Tiger Mother. The Pearl Concubine got tossed down the well like yesterday's garbage.

I recall this bit of Chinese history to remind myself that servitude can bring satisfaction, but it's also a bottomless pit. If you aren't careful, it can be the wishing well that you throw yourself down, and no one will climb in to save you. The sides are slippery. While you try to get a foothold as a woman, and as a mother, you might find yourself in that pit of despair and not know how to pull yourself out.

So before you get there, you have to stop yourself. You have one life to live, and it is yours.

By then I knew I'd never be a Tiger Mom, but it hadn't occurred to me that I was susceptible to the drowned-girl-in-a-well scenario. Realistically, the modern-day equivalent would be to drown oneself over a period of years in bottomless vodka cocktails, but I won't be doing that either.

I am a marshmallow Peep. I will not be "toughening up" any-time soon. However, nor will I be crying at the dinner table if the food isn't perfect or because I've burdened myself with endless people pleasing. From now on, I'll be who I am and relinquish control of all the things I can't possibly manipulate into seamless perfection.

The Hot Mess Club just isn't for me. I hereby tender my res-ignation.

28

Dispatches from the Front Lines of Third Grade

Growing up as an Asian American person, you are often called on to explain or defend your race. Even if you are too young to have the confidence or vocabulary to stand up for yourself, situations arise that make you feel crummy, and that uneasy feeling can linger from early childhood up through adulthood.

By nine years old, my daughter has already encountered disparaging comments about Chinese people. She has witnessed games and scenarios played out by kids younger than she and overheard phrases such as "Look at my Chinese hat. I'm a funny Chinaman!" and "I'm a Chinese girl," accompanied by mincing steps and the stretching sideways of the eyelids to make slanty eyes. My daughter told me about these incidences that transpired on the playground and after school. The words were not necessarily directed at her, but hearing them and seeing other kids laugh made her feel lousy. She is proud to be Chinese, and hence, she was confused as to why these imitations of Chinese people were deemed so hilarious.

How do I prevent my kid from internalizing shame for something that is not her fault? I am not proud to have done so, but when I was younger, I myself occasionally laughed along with hurtful comments or remained silent to avoid being targeted next for derision. But my daughter is just a kid. How is she supposed to feel, and what should I say to her?

I don't want to lecture her about Chinese American history or make her feel worse than she already does, but I also don't want to ignore her feelings either. I want to validate that she is right to question mimicry and jokes that mock others. I sometimes suggest phrases she might say, such as "It's not okay to make fun of people," but I know that at her age and with her nonconfrontational personality, she would rather keep quiet. Also, I know that little kids make fun of everybody and anybody, and I don't want to make a mountain out of a molehill.

Nonetheless, if I don't say something, who will? I could initiate the whole teacher conference thing and drag in the alleged offenders, but have you ever been involved in one of these kinds of meetings with multiple parents, kids, and teachers? The sessions quickly devolve into a he said–she said squabble, with parents often getting apoplectic, and kids even defending their tormentors. It can be a pretty big mess, so one must carefully consider if the offending joke, gesture, or glance is really worth hauling in all the involved parties who are just going to end up fuming and blaming one another.

Instead, Lucy and I usually just talk to each other in private. And although my husband definitely has the right to be included, sometimes I don't tell him of every little disturbance because he will feel the most outraged of us all. I don't need him stomping his gigantic, steaming-mad self up some unsuspecting parent's driveway like an albino Incredible Hulk only to get his head blown off with a shotgun.

But, yes, we talk. Not in a big, family meeting kind of way, but just as we're walking to school, or making lunch, or whenever an in-between time allows us a few quiet moments. I don't want to act so riled up or hurt that Lucy actually just stops telling me stuff. If I were a kid, that's precisely what I would do. I'd feel so bummed already, and if I knew that my parent would be further upset by what I had to say, I'd just stop talking. So with that in mind, I don't fly into a rage, even if that's what I'm feeling. Our talks about teasing, and particularly about race, are hard to have. But I want to keep having them. In emotional housekeeping, sometimes the hardest work of all is to not sweep things under the carpet.

A little while ago, my daughter was sitting in the bathtub and I was brushing my teeth when she started to tell me about a play that students in an older grade performed at her school. It was about the history of California, and Lucy said she hated the part where a Chinese gold miner got beaten up. Her initial description was that the "Chinese" kid got beat up and everyone laughed, which made her really angry.

"Was it really a Chinese kid?"

"No, a blond boy dressed up like he was Chinese."

"And what do you mean he was beaten up?"

"It was supposed to be pretend," she said, starting to get upset. "But it was mean."

"Well, yes, Chinese miners up here did get beaten up a lot, and it was unfair and mean. It is true that that did happen . . ."

"But everybody didn't have to laugh!" she exclaimed, and then burst into tears.

Oh. I hadn't really anticipated having a conversation about discrimination, racism, and violence against Chinese people when she was still so young, but here we were. Meanwhile, I was thinking of all the regular parent things, like getting her out of the bathtub, drying her hair, clipping her fingernails, putting her to bed, transferring the laundry into the dryer, and so on.

But then something distracted me, like the phone rang or something. We somehow dropped the subject, I got her out of the tub, and we resumed our bedtime routine. Shortly thereafter, Rolf came upstairs to read to her, and I went downstairs to finish the dishes.

I forgot all about our bathtime conversation until the next morning. I was lying on my foam mat stretching because I feel about ninety years old if I don't exercise, when suddenly I remembered what Lucy had said about the school play. From my curled-up position on the floor, I shot upright and thought, *WTF?* I was alone, so I felt the freedom to be completely angry now. I paced and tried to figure out what to do. I seethed. I had to find out what really happened.

Be calm, I told myself. I wanted to honor that my kid felt angry, but I also knew that kids get upset about a lot of things that eventually fizzle out. Also, it was possible that maybe her perception was not exactly how things had happened. I wanted to give the people in charge the benefit of the doubt. And yet. When you see your own daughter sad and hurt, you want to lash out. But here was a situation where someone had to be the adult, and in our household, that responsibility does not fall to the little one who's playing with a mermaid Polly Pocket.

So I called the school. I asked a woman there whom I trust if she had seen the play. I didn't want to accuse. I didn't want to rush right out the gate foaming at the mouth. I wanted to catch more flies with honey than with vinegar. (Once I caught the flies, then I could burn their bodies in a vat of industrial-strength acid.)

I carefully described the situation and admitted that I wasn't sure what to do exactly, but felt that I did need to do *something*. This longtime educator and member of the school community suggested that if a kid, any kid, felt that strong of a negative reaction, the teachers putting on the play should at least know about it.

So I hung up the phone and decided to e-mail the teachers. An hour later, when I arrived at the school for pickup, a kind of buzz had already occurred. Apparently, the recipients of my e-mail had already forwarded my message to others. Several teachers and parents pulled me aside to offer their support. Two were glad I had said something, and another expressed relief. Another opined, "I think it's great that you stand up for what you believe in."

I hadn't expected anyone else to read that e-mail, nor did I think that word would travel so fast. After I met Lucy in front of her classroom, we walked up to the corner where I knew the teacher who'd organized the play performed afternoon cross-walk duty.

Once we got talking, I was glad I had given him the benefit of the doubt before I charged at him with accusations. He described the scene to me and offered to show me the script for my opinion and input. We ended up having an extensive conversation about California history, early relations between the Irish and Chinese, institutionalized racism, and the teaching of children at different grade levels.

I was happy that Lucy was witness to the fact that we don't have to bury our feelings. We can confront them.

For many weeks after this incident, the whole experience stayed with me. I thought about the quiet way Lucy brought this subject to my attention, how I had forgotten about it because daily life had distracted me, and then how irate I had become despite simultaneously being unsure of myself. I thought about how difficult it is to separate one's child's feelings from one's own.

I surmised that if I were my grandma Ruby on my dad's side, I would have not said or done anything. I would have "not made trouble." And if I were my grandma Lucy on my mom's side, I would've blown my stack immediately and would've been heard shouting from blocks away. My grannies had two very different approaches to handling disagreements. Maybe throughout my childhood I had observed and absorbed the various effects of these two ways of Chinese being—deferential as a matter of survival, versus hotheaded to one's own detriment—and having witnessed these two disparate ways of interacting with the world, I realized that neither way felt right for me.

The trick in standing up for oneself is to do so without having to step on someone else. All in all, I was glad I had handled this incident at school in my own way.

For some reason, this incident reminded me of an obituary I'd read several years ago for the actress Miyoshi Umeki. In it, one of her costars from the past had mentioned that he had at one time attempted to contact Umeki, but he couldn't find an address or number for her anywhere, and that no one else he'd asked knew of her whereabouts. I remember the words in the article, "She did not want to be found."

She did not want to be found. I had remembered thinking that that strategy sounded very reasonable. Umeki had been a big star for many years and was the first and only Asian to win a Best Supporting Actress Academy Award, for 1957's *Sayonara*. She was one of the main characters in 1961's *Flower Drum Song*, but I knew her mostly as Mrs. Livingston on *The Courtship of Eddie's Father*. I can only imagine what kind of treatment she encountered as one of Hollywood's most prominent Asian stars, particularly in an era that spanned World War II with intense anti-Japanese sentiment.

I began to think about how, in a way, I hadn't wanted to be found either. After living in hyperpoliticized San Francisco and Berkeley, where race awareness is always set on DEFCON 1, my own experiences with racial slights, weird looks, well-meaning yet nonetheless irritating remarks, and occasional outright hostility had worn me out. I had wanted to move away because, frankly, my nerves were shot.

The Bay Area is so politicized that everywhere you go, you signify something to someone. American-born or fresh-off-the-boat? Speak Chinese or English? Married or single? Gay or straight? Kids or dogs? Bike or car? Omnivore or herbivore? Lacto-ovo or vegan? Butch or femme? Democrat or Republican? Working mother or stay-at-home mom?

I needed a respite from soaking in racial controversy 24/7, a break from a life where going to Walgreens and buying tampons once attracted an old Chinese lady who took it upon herself to inform me that "only stupid and no respect American Chinese use tampon because don't care about virgin."

Moving from San Francisco to Nevada City, I thought I didn't want to be found, but something sure found me. Speaking up about that scene in the play changed me.

Our daily tasks are many, and it's easy to blow stuff off, especially small things that we can convince ourselves are no big deal. But this was a big deal. It was one detail in life's myriad details, but it showed me that if someone like me—fairly educated, outgoing, physically able—feels the pull of inertia, then what about people whose obstacles are pronounced? How unsure of themselves must they be? And if I don't speak up, who will?

That small confrontation about the school play was a turning point in my development as an adult. It made me realize I couldn't cower. I'm forty-three, and tired. My body had been taken apart and put back together through pregnancy, and having written three novels about growing up Chinese American, I've been snickered at, chided, figuratively spat on, and had arrows pointed at me. Nonetheless, I can't just hide out and hope not to be found.

Tiger Babies, I'm done cowering.

PART 5

Older and Wiser

29

Mommy,
I Know What the F-Word Is!

Is it . . . flummox?

I am a Tiger Mom only in that my back is killing me so I'm covered in Tiger Balm patches, smelling supersexy. Forty is the new eighty.

My goal for my daughter is a normal childhood, with more fun than I ever had. In pursuit of the hearth and home I want, I don't aim to replicate the fantasy of Norman Rockwell paintings, or even *Brady Bunch* episodes; rather, for our little family I just want safety, good times, and love.

Instead of overscheduling every moment of the week, I think it's important to have time just to sit and stare at a tree. If you are Chinese, you just read that and thought, *Yes, but couldn't you do calculus at the same time?*

As my kid would say, "Missing the point!"

Sometimes we just sit on the couch and hug each other. She might say, in her guileless way, "I just want to lie here and squeeze your fat."

Don't you mean 100 percent muscle?

I've read that brain development needs fat. Yes, in one's diet, and also squeezing your loved ones' fat. We're happy as clams. (Yeah, until she doesn't get into Harvard, then we'll see who's happy . . .)

In any case, we have a lot of "at home" afternoons and weekends, and that's what we like. I am glad we make time just to hang around each other and do nothing. But it's really not as easy as you might think. It's a conscious decision to do less, not more. And this choice is not about laziness.

It takes a certain kind of discipline to carve out time to be together, doing what looks like nothing. For me it's the first step in showing Lucy how we are the only ones responsible for hollowing out our own inner space to think. I've learned that no one is ever going to say it's okay to sit and stare at the sky. Maybe no authority figure is ever going to give you permission to do what you want to do with your life. Whether it's looking at the clouds, becoming a writer, or making some other big decision for yourself, no one else will ease your distractions or definitively tell you, "Now is the time."

Also, I don't want Lucy to feel like she is constantly being shuttled from place to place. I've learned that lesson from other parents, and other kids as well. One particular sentence uttered by my niece sticks in my mind. Someone asked her, "Where do you live?"

And without missing a beat, she replied, "I live in the car."

I don't want Lucy to live in the car.

A Tiger Mom might say, "What, are you aiming for mediocrity?"

Not at all. I'm striving to excel in the things I consider crucial to becoming an excellent human being, in all such categories not measured in grades or test scores, unquantifiable in awards or number of fake friends on Facebook. My husband and I are attempting the slow, cumulative work of exemplifying compassion, kindness, and gratitude. It's an incremental, drawn-out, marching-ever-forward process to teach your kid to be true to her word, and to figure out what it means to have personal integrity. Thoughtful explanations take time, and in accelerated Adult Land there is already too little of that, as everyone knows. We need cleared space in our heads so that we may listen for the clues from a kid's interior world. My daughter's concerns are expressed like tiny yelps from Whoville, and I feel that if I'm not already listening for it, the small voice will be lost in the background noise of homework, dancing lessons, swim class, and everything else.

And you bet I'd sometimes rather be doing things other than living in the mind-set of a nine-year-old. Cuz, really, how much more can I possibly talk about Garfield, listen to knock-knock jokes, and write haikus about kittens? But someone has got to do it, and that someone is me. My brain would much rather be reading *The New Yorker,* but instead we're building a spaceship out of plastic scraps and paper towels for her school's egg-dropping contest. She has named her raw egg "Captain Yolkandwhites," and he is going to be tossed off the school roof in the morning. If the egg breaks, so will her little heart, and that ain't gonna happen on my watch.

I am in the trenches with recycled bubble wrap and Elmer's

glue. It's where I need to be. Frankly, it can be a royal pain. But I've got to stay flexible, shift gears, and constantly rethink my own mental state if I'm going to preserve my kid's bright-eyed love of life, her natural exuberance, and her ability to enjoy watching the clouds moving ever so slowly.

From the moment Lucy was born, I looked into her eyes and whispered, "I see you."

When I was a kid, that's all I ever wanted to hear, to know in my heart. I wanted to know that someone saw who I was inside, but instead, my family focused only on practical matters: get in the car, eat your dinner, finish your homework, write your thank-you notes, don't be late for school, practice your piano, get to basketball practice, and so forth.

After I participated in all my activities, and obeyed all the rules, when would anyone ever see who I was, or ask what I'd like or what I wanted?

Every obligation we rushed off to. Every family event where my accomplishments or failures were discussed in detail as if I wasn't sitting right there, I was always wondering, *Can we just go home now?* And even when we did get home, I wondered, *Can I just be myself now?* Would I ever have time just to stare into space and try to figure out exactly what that might be?

Sure. Just as soon as you get into UC Berkeley. I mean, after you graduate. Oops, my bad. I meant graduate in four years with a double major. Of course, with honors. That goes without saying if you are Chinese.

When I look at my own daughter, I think back to my own childhood and wonder, was I ever really satisfied or happy with straight As and piano recitals? I know I was satisfied to have pleased someone else. I wasn't actually ever discovering for myself what I really liked, nor had I been asked. Of course, if I *had* been asked, I would have said I liked puffy stickers and touching "down there." Good Lord! Better double up on those piano lessons to keep those nimble fingers busy!

Oh, and speaking of the Lord, I was mighty afraid of hell. Because I attended Catholic school, I lost a lot of sleep before the age of ten, worrying if the next two dimes I swiped off the kitchen counter were going to be the last drips of Christ's blood to overflow the world's chalice full of sins. I worried about mortal sins and venial sins, memorized lengthy prayers and couplets out of my Chinese school textbooks, only to parrot everything back to teachers without understanding what they meant.

I was a good learner, a real homework machine. I spent my waking hours doing precisely what I'd been told so I would avoid both everlasting hell and, potentially the next worse thing, paltry acceptance into only a junior college. In retrospect, between St. Brigid's School and a Chinese upbringing, I had a lot of worry I didn't need to have. I could have been running through a forest or feeling the sunshine on my skin. But I had learned early that fresh air was only for suckers who didn't get in to Berkeley.

Which is so not true. Once I got to college, there were plenty of people who'd grown up swimming and playing, and generally had had a grand time. And here we were, having ended up at the same school. I probably could've gone to the beach more and would have still gotten into the same college. I could've taken off my shoes and socks more during the first twenty years of my life. For Pete's sake, I wasn't even supposed to walk around without socks *in our house.*

Yep, coulda lived a little more on the edge.

But hey, cry me a river made of Purell. Lucy is plenty bare-foot during the summer and catches snowflakes on her tongue in the winter. She stomps in mud and swims, plays with roly-poly bugs, has friends who live right next door, and has me to pick her up from school every day.

I am aware that my parents were working hard for me and making sacrifices of their own, but when I saw moms on TV baking cookies and actually talking to their kids, I always yearned to know what that might be like. I had wanted that so bad, and now I have the opportunity to give that to my own child. I am able to give her a mother who spends time with her, who sees who she is now and who she is becoming. I am her unequivocal ally through life.

And as such, I am the opposite of a Tiger Mom. I actively choose to not constantly pressure my child to do better, as if who and what she is isn't good enough. I strive not to make her feel like I am consistently disappointed in her. I am not sham-ing her into excelling by calling her names like "garbage."

So sue me.

And in twenty years, let's hope my daughter doesn't.

Hopefully, she will remember how I put my brain aside for several years in order to play with her creepy, freaky Care Bears. In case you don't know, Care Bears appear cuddly and cheery, but their secret agenda is to melt the adult brain. In their world, if you can't get fired up about painting a cloud with a rainbow-dipped brush, they collectively focus their zombie eyes at you and hypnotize away your bad behavior in a mind-control ex-periment known as the Care Bear Stare. I know these things because I have crawled on the floor for hours, setting up tea parties for Tender Heart Bear, Bashful Heart, Funshine, America Cares, and Perfect & Polite Panda. Believe me, I wanted to snuff them all out with an Uzi that shoots fire like the gun Ripley uses in *Aliens*. But instead I usually place two Cheerios each on their tiny plates as my daughter pours water into their teacups.

When I think of the Tiger Mom parenting style, in which playdates are forbidden and carelessly drawn birthday cards are refused as inferior, I don't imagine a lot of parent participation in crawling around on the floor like a Care Bear. That sounds so much easier for the parent, but I don't know how it is for the kid. I couldn't ever say no to the sound of my child begging, "Mommy, play with me, pleeeeeaaase!"

One of the saddest sounds I ever heard was when Lucy was two years old, standing in our hallway on the other side of the door where I was inside the bedroom writing. I was on a book deadline and was trying to concentrate, trying to forget the dirty dishes, willing myself to put domestic concerns out of my mind. Meanwhile, Lucy was pounding on the door with her wee little fists sobbing, "Mommy . . . Mommy . . . Mommy . . ." I could see her little stocking feet stomping like two Jazzercising blobs of cookie dough through the crack between the floor and the bottom of the door. As she exhausted herself screaming my name, she sank lower and lower until she was lying prone like an exhausted meatloaf. The lump on the other side of the door whimpered, "Maaa-maaa."

I wanted to die. I stopped what I was doing, opened the door, and scooped her off the floor. She came to life like the happy baby I knew her to be, and I let her mash my face with her hands to her heart's content. From then on, I told myself, she could have a desk next to mine, and I would teach her how to work quietly, or else I would have to work at night while she slept. That pounding on the door thing accompanied by uncontrollable sobs was just too heartbreaking. I vowed that I would never keep a locked door between us again.

30

Dismantling the Lonely Honeycomb of Your Inner Wasp's Nest

I want Lucy to have access to everything I didn't have, and by that I mean barefoot summers and afternoons of digging in the sand or swimming at the nearby pool. She needs the chance to get dirty, to meet other kids, and to goof around for no other purpose than to have fun. We've chosen a life for her that includes neighborhood friends, walks to and from school, and relaxing days in the backyard watering flowers. We've created a slower pace of living, with less rule following and more looking at the clouds. In contrast, my upbringing was scheduled in every increment, and I don't want to revisit that upon my own daughter.

But make no mistake. I am a very attentive mother. When Lucy was an infant, I would let her sit and stare at me for long chunks of time, and I did not look away. When she wailed inconsolably for no apparent reason, I gently bounced her and told her, "I love you even when you're crying. It's okay to be sad. I love you even when you are sad . . ." It helped a lot, this mantra. It kept me from going insane especially when I was so frustrated that I would have rather jabbed myself in the eye with a Mr. Potato Head arm than to have the crying go on and on. Which it did. The crying scrambled my brain. But what else could I do?

In addition, I strive to be particularly gentle and attentive when tending to her personal care such as washing and grooming. I remember my own mom ripping a comb through by hair so hard that the comb's *metal* teeth *broke off*. She'd continue to rake the jagged, broken points through my tangles as I screamed. I had always promised myself there would be none of that for Lucy.

So here we are. You can call me a coddling, permissive parent, but also, when it comes to food, I don't even mind making a separate kid dinner for Lucy. It doesn't take that much more time, and I'm not interested in misery at the dinner table or an endless battle of wills that can be solved easily with a piece of whole-grain bread, a little cream cheese, and some strawberries. In my experience as a parent, drawing lines in the sand that you decree you will never cross, sooner or later, makes ya kinda look like an idiot. So I'll just make burritos *and* mac 'n' cheese and call it good.

And over here we're playdate central. We've got neighborhood munchkins dressed as ladybugs and bumblebees. We're digging deep, muddy channels in the backyard. We're saving the lives of every roly-poly bug we find. Our hands are busy making ghosts out of paper napkins and washed-out yogurt cups, and we're transforming milk cartons into cars with paint and the wheels from an old stroller. Countless grilled cheese sandwiches have been consumed, and we've cleaned hundreds of sticky fingers, milk mustaches, and muddy little feet. Sometimes the hair is a little messy, but so far, the world hasn't ended.

I'm not striving for competitive perfection for Lucy. Instead, I'm seeking excellence in a different way. In ways nobody might be able to see, measure, or quantify. I'm teaching Lucy the subtleties of listening to her own body, and her own heart. We are helping her to talk about her emotions. We want her to be a happy kid. We want her to be a good friend, to play fair, and to be a compassionate and kind person. We do not refuse hugs.

So how can we be careful and attentive, without turning into banshee fascists from Crazytown? I understand that when both parents work full-time, and have their feet firmly planted in the adult world, it can be really difficult to shift gears and set one's mind to Shrinky Dinks level. But I have time to do it, and the desire, also. Of course, it does require being once again in between two worlds, between pretending you're Hunka Munka the mouse and, say, itemizing bills from one's healthcare provider. Keeping up with the fast-paced, seemingly nonsensical minds of several five- or nine-year-olds while cooking and cleaning up after them, and constantly stepping on every last Polly Pocket, Perler bead, and Webkinz, will fry both your brain and your body. Meanwhile, your adult responsibilities still have a raygun pointed to your head.

To give ourselves a break, we make the conscious decision to not be overscheduled. I'm not sure when simply being together and talking to each other became a luxury. Even if you take the kid out of the equation and are only referring to communication with one's spouse, it's so easy for a wall of work, chores, daily routines, and family duties to come between us. Sometimes we're both so exhausted that it's more convenient just to slump our aching bodies against this invisible wall of fatigue and inertia instead of tearing it down. This wall is not a physical wall, and yet it has everything to do with all the material detritus of our cluttered lives: old PG&E bill stubs, dead computers, and stacks of paperwork taking up room in the corner, and hundreds of white plastic bags shoved in drawers.

And if you have kids, add to this barrier the other piles of stuff that accumulate everywhere. Our mental and emotional flexibility is further hindered by the heaps of dirty clothes, stuffed animals, clean socks, drawings that we can't bear to throw away, old books, crushed tissue boxes, and maybe a Ziploc bag containing two squished grapes. Haystacks of that stuff add to the aforementioned wall of psychological ennui, and one can feel so stuck that one can barely muster the energy to watch the pet-fur tumbleweeds roll by.

This wall is the weight-bearing infrastructure of a lonely house of cards. If we are not vigilant about monitoring this wall's proliferation, it gets bulkier every day until the space between us is so massive that it divides the rooms we inhabit, and eventually every room. The wall multiplies into many partitions until it's a honeycomb in which every family member is in his or her own cubicle. The structure becomes tighter and more constricting, and the honey that oozes from it tastes slightly rancid. Who wants to be a lonely queen bee, anyway?

So to avoid this honeycomb of loneliness, my spouse and I are constantly attempting to disassemble this invisible, quiet, insidious wall.

Sometimes it can feel like bailing water out of a rowboat with a Dixie cup.

Achievement, shmeevment. If we don't even see each other, or like each other anymore, what's the point? It's easy to hide behind a things-to-do list to avoid everyone you live with, including yourself.

And I don't want that to happen to us. But it already has, several times. Sometimes a few days, weeks, or even months can go by without getting to the Abstract Wall Dismantling Project. It's an ongoing process, and the wall can get built up again seemingly overnight, like a wasps' nest under the eaves.

But we keep chipping away at it, little by little. It takes conscious concentration to make sure airholes are effectively poked through the wall cells to keep us from getting crushed by our own bulky behemoth of busy schedules and heaps of benign mess.

I keep one eye on the state of the wall at all times to make sure it's not getting out of control. Meanwhile, not every success can be measured on a perforated test sheet or typed-out report card. At the beginning, middle, and end of each day, I always want to see my daughter's funny little smile.

31

Don't Wash Pinky, Okay?

Just recently I came to the realization that my grandma Lucy was much kinder to me than she ever was to my mother. I never recognized that when I was younger. It is only in watching the interaction between my own daughter and mother that I've even stopped to consider what my mother's relationship with her own mom was. I see a pattern here. Just as Grandma Lucy was hard on my mom but sweet to me, likewise, my mother has never been warm and fuzzy in my experience, but to my daughter she's as cuddly as a kitten.

When Chinese babies are born, it is a tradition to dress them in animal-motif hats and booties, usually representing pigs or tigers. The idea is to trick evil spirits into thinking that the precious baby is actually just a common piglet or other such lowly creature, hardly worth stealing away. It makes me wonder if Chinese parents' constant putting down of their children is related to this custom. Thus, no matter how good-looking or smart your children are, it's always best not to call attention to them. Maybe that's why, even if you are highly accomplished, your parent will always treat you like a humble worm.

My mother has always been a beauty, but my grandma Lucy's way of handing out selective compliments distorted my mom's self-image. My mom says, "Jeannette was the pretty one. I was always so ugly!" Even when my mother and I flip through her wedding album, she refers to herself as "ugly." And when I hear her say that, I can't believe it. In every photo she looks absolutely gorgeous. It makes me sad to think my mother has gone through life not knowing how pretty she is.

However, with Chinese parents, no compliment seems to go unpunished. Grandma Lucy often praised my aunt as the pretty one, but often also commented that she had no common sense. So she was good-looking but dumb. And in this same style of distorted logic, my grandmother calling my mom "ugly" was perhaps meant as a backhanded way of calling her smart. It was obviously not an actual compliment of any kind, but rather some type of cultural one-two punch that continued the long tradition of parental withholding. And we all know it's only the bad stuff that sticks. So my mom only heard "ugly" and that was that.

As a young teen my mother had a job in a Chinatown shop, and she describes her boss as having been a very kind woman who never got mad at her. She recounted a story about an incident in which she dropped a very expensive tea set, and it smashed into a hundred pieces. The boss reassured her it was an accident and didn't even make her pay for the broken porcelain. My mother has said of the woman, "I wished that she was my mother."

When my mom told me this story, I almost fell out of my chair. I thought, *Whaaat? Grandma Lucy was such a loving, doting grandmother to me, so how is Mom saying she wished someone else was her mom?*

My mother went on. "If I had dropped something like that at home and it broke like that, Pau Pau would have pulled my ears and screamed at me."

Hmmm. As I mulled over this story in my mind and compared it to the grandmother I knew, I couldn't imagine my pau pau ever pulling my ears or hurting me in any way. She doted on me always; she prepared all my favorite foods, bathed me, and even made mundane trips to the grocery store seem fun. She always made me feel loved. So what did this mean that she didn't bestow this same affection on my own mother?

Are grandmothers nicer to grandkids because they know they weren't necessarily stellar parents and are trying to make up for it? Are they taking full advantage of getting a second chance at child rearing?

Or are they guilt-ridden and trying to cover up for past deeds by pretending that they've always been sweet as pie? Maybe if they pamper the babies of the previously scorned child, might decades-old sins be forgiven?

Instead of the direct route of just saying sorry, which would require losing face, maybe if the grandmother wins over the heart of the grandchild, she can maintain the position that she is right, and always has been. By doting on the next generation, a grandmother demonstrates, "Look how nice I am, and have always been! If you recall anything different, that's your problem." This strategy possesses a built-in mechanism: the adult child will be made to feel like she's crazy if she claims to remember anything bad about her own childhood. This shell game switcheroo is considered no biggie unless, of course, you are the one being made to feel crazy.

Did any of this unconscious motivation factor into Grandma Lucy's behavior? Maybe she hoped my mother would forgive and forget that she'd had her ears pulled and was made to feel ugly.

Or perhaps my grandmother simply mellowed with age. I feel guilty and slightly ashamed to even be speculating that anything other than affection compelled her actions. I know Grandma Lucy's love for me was real. Nonetheless, apparently, this certainty does not squelch my compulsive need to fish through my memories in search of clues.

Now that Grandma Lucy has passed away, and many years separate me from my childhood, I will never know the many subtleties of my mom's relationship with her own mother. I don't have too many sharp memories of them together; if we were all in the same room it was because we were at big parties with lots of people around. When I did see my mother and grandmother talking, it was always of practical matters, and half the time in Chinese. Mostly, though, it hadn't occurred to me then to pay any attention to the way *they* interacted.

I liked being alone with my grandmother best, just the two of us. We often found ourselves solely in each other's company because my grandfather, parents, and older brothers were always busy doing other things. I was too young to be stirring up trouble with my own friends just yet, and she seemed to enjoy quiet evenings when she wasn't playing mah-jongg.

However, I do recall that my grandma Lucy used to say insidious, disparaging things to me about my mom. While Grandma Lucy and I ate Chinese dishes that she had prepared fresh and piping hot, she would make comments such as "Your ma never cook Chinese food," and "She only give you cold thing like sandwich." My grandmother would speak with obvious disdain and disapproval. I knew not to disagree with her, even though I knew there was nothing wrong with how we ate at home.

In retrospect, I wonder if this was Grandma Lucy's way of bonding with me. Once again using a distorted logic, maybe my grandmother bad-mouthed my mom to me so that we could feel separate from her and thereby somehow closer to each other as grandmother and granddaughter. Perhaps these statements were a way of saying, "Stick with me because I know how to love you best," or "Whatever happens, don't forget me." Maybe with age, a grandmother feels closer to her own mortality. Hence, she does what she can to ensure that she is cherished, and remembered.

I recognize this dynamic because now a similar pattern plays out with my own mom and daughter. While I know full well that my mother used to comb my hair with ferocious, painful zeal, she is gentle with Lucy. When my daughter was younger, my mom was always careful in helping her with her socks and shoes, and I've witnessed none of the rough tugging on of clothes and heard none of the sharp tones of voice that had been the norm for me.

My mother and Lucy don't see each other on a daily basis, and of course, it is in rushing to school, doing difficult home-work, and when everyone's tired that frustration and bickering are most likely to erupt. So maybe it's the schedule of their mostly weekend and vacation time together that contributes to their more easygoing interactions.

But that can't be everything. Granted, my mother is retired now and her life is about ten times less hectic than it ever was when she was working full-time and taking care of three kids.

For whatever combination of reasons, she is more patient and kind than she was with me when I was Lucy's age. I am not jealous, just simply damn glad.

However. (There is always a however, right?)

There are signs of the same kind of conspiratorial conversation between my mom and Lucy that occurred between Grandma Lucy and me. My mom, to my knowledge, doesn't bag on my cooking, but there are other things.

For instance, a few years ago, my parents took Lucy on an overnight trip to the coast. A few days after they returned, Lucy and I were sitting on the couch playing with her favorite bear, Pinky, and as she clutched the soft toy to her chest, she placed her head on my lap and said, "Why does Pau Pau think you're lazy?"

"What do you mean?" I asked. Lucy sat up and stared at Pinky, who was faded, well loved, and so worn and soft that the plush, fake fur was looking as if it might rip at any time. One tumble in the washing machine could be the end of her.

"Well, Pau Pau was looking at Pinky. She asked me why she was so dirty. When I said I didn't know, she said it was because you're lazy and you don't wash her."

"Really, she said that?"

"I don't want you to wash her! Don't wash Pinky, okay? Pau Pau says you're lazy, but you're not lazy. You're doing stuff all the time. Why does she say things like that?"

"I don't know."

A little while later, I phoned my mom and called her on the mat.

"Hello?"

"Did you tell Lucy that I'm lazy because I didn't wash her stuffed animal?"

"No, I never said that."

"Well, Lucy wouldn't lie about that. And she doesn't want it washed. Why would you tell her I'm lazy? Now she just thinks you're a liar."

That part about my mom being a liar was kind of harsh, I know, but I was mad. Why would she criticize me to my own kid? We went back and forth a few times, but my mom continued to deny that she had told my daughter that I was lazy. We hung up the phone without resolution.

Maybe a grandmother feels like she has to vie for the attention of the grandchild. Maybe these little digs are the only way to express simmering envy that daughters have more opportunities for jobs or love, or are younger and have numerous other advantages. Maybe a fine line exists between all the conflicting emotions that arise: you want your kid to succeed, but not too much, or you want her to have a life full of love, but if it seems that she has it all too easy, that burns you.

Perhaps, as an individual, the grandmother feels underappreciated. Or maybe she is secretly afraid that her value is slipping in the eyes of the next generation, and she must bolster up her own reputation. As if I didn't already know it, Grandma Lucy would often exclaim to me, "My soup is the best!" These pronouncements would even sometimes be made in the third person, as if someone else were affirming these truths. "Pau Pau's *tong mien* is the best!" she would say. She needed me to physically nod and agree although, as previously noted, my own mother never cooked Chinese food, so the comparison was already a victory by default. Nonetheless, when it came to declaring superiority, just like a Chinese person, with Grandma Lucy there was no such thing as gilding the lily.

For her entire life, my own mother hasn't ever been lazy.

It's true that she never had a time in her life where she had the luxury of acting, being, or doing anything frivolously. By comparison, I did have free time. I've had the opportunity to enjoy college, work friends, and several kid-free years of marriage. But that doesn't make me lazy, for heaven's sake.

I know that my mother is happy for me. And yet. There have always been little comments here and there, such as "Rolf is such a hard worker," and "Rolf is so good at cleaning." These compliments serve the alternate purpose of insinuating that I am neither a hard worker nor good at cleaning. My mom also tells my husband, "She's so lucky she found you."

Ah, there's that Chinese adherence to the concept of "luck." I could enumerate all the difficulties, setbacks, false starts, and hard times my husband and I have worked through that are certainly not just simply luck. We have both worked hard, and neither of us is lazy. But here we are. Under the umbrella of Luck, in one fell swoop all our collective efforts, painstaking struggles, anguish, and hard-earned accomplishments can be disregarded by a Tiger Mom.

Maybe I need to compliment my mother more. I don't know. We all want to feel more appreciated, and more loved. That wish doesn't diminish, no matter what one's age is. Everyone wants and needs more compliments and praise whether she is two, nine, twenty, forty, or seventy years old. I don't mind giving sincere recognition to my loved ones.

Thanks, Mom. You've done a great job and continue to do so. But please do not disparage me to my own daughter.

You are not ugly. I am not lazy. And for goodness' sake, please do not wash Pinky.

32

Before You Vanish Out of View

I recently went back to San Francisco for the holidays. For dinner we had a culinary mash-up of cultures: sushi appetizers, a huge turkey stuffed with Chinese sticky rice, prawns with Vietnamese hot sauce, a sautéed veggie medley with *siew choy,* black mushrooms, and pea pods. No one knew what to buy anyone for Christmas so we all exchanged Nordstrom gift cards.

After eating, we did what I suppose many families in the United States do, we passed out on the sofa and watched *The Godfather* trilogy on whatever channel was playing it. Knowing all the dialogue in these movies took the place of actual talking, but strangely enough, sharing the familiar lines had its own kind of intimacy. I watched Vito Corleone as a boy at Ellis Island and thought of my own grandfather Lemuel Jen at Angel Island as a child. I'd seen this movie so many times that whenever I tried to imagine my grandfather's arrival in America, all I ever pictured was this scene from this movie.

My parents, siblings, and our spouses all sat around, eating a little more, and grazing over dessert. We were all lost in our own thoughts as we rested there, not talking.

After helping with the dishes and saying good night to everyone, it was suddenly 11:30 P.M. in San Francisco. I got ready for bed as a visitor in my parents' house, as a guest in my childhood bedroom. The night sky was clear with a few white, puffy clouds. I could smell the trees in Golden Gate Park even though I had a cold. It was more that I could *feel* the smells and sounds in the way a blind person can see just fine. Like a forked branch divining water, I felt San Francisco reverberating in my bones.

I was shaking like that. Shaking with the colors and patterns, the paisleys and toiles, the fragrances natural or manufactured, the rough touches and smooth caresses of the spirit of the city. I could hear the urban whispers through the airplane-head of my cold.

Was that how you were luring me back, San Francisco, by getting into my head? I imagined a conversation between us:

Come back to me.

I will, Mom, but you've got to stop suffocating me.

I almost got to you with that thick aroma of éclairs and pastries from Tartine, didn't I?

Yes. I'm a nervous wreck when I'm living with you. You have too much power over me and your embrace crushes my bones.

But I don't crush your spirit, do I?

No, never.

Then get back here. Now.

That wasn't too subtle. What about finesse?

You're just being a brat. Come home.

Not yet. Let me admire you, San Fran, from this short distance. Remember how I used to be so nearsighted? Now I'm farsighted, and the only way I can really see you is if I hold you at arm's length, like a book.

And you wonder why you're so lonely, kid.

I know it's my own fault.

I'm the one with fault lines.

No, San Francisco, those are laugh lines.

Dear city, you are my Underdog secret energy pill. My photographic memory is turned on like a spotlight. I can't help but bank every image, every step across the marble floor of the Veterans Building or City Hall, the glitter silica in the downtown squares of pavement. In my mind's eye I can see the destroyed Chinatown that the current Chinatown is paved over. I see the ghost-gone Victorians behind the '60s-era office buildings. I remember the old places that were barely standing in the backdrops of *The Streets of San Francisco.*

Seeing these city apparitions takes a certain clairvoyance, and San Franciscans often perceive the images of the past with the mysterious vision of a third eye, like on the pyramid on the back of the one-dollar bill. Their ears are attuned to hear confessions in what's not said. As for their sense of smell and memory, the purpose of perfume, after all, is to disguise odors, so what lingers after the floral notes have evaporated? In the wind off the ocean, the old smells can still be a revelation when one suddenly catches a whiff again. You might get a subtle, new-grass smell or the aroma of baked goods from a nearby bakery. I remember the pungent coffee smell from the Hills Bros. Coffee Building, and recall breathing in a hint of grape soda when we drove by the Shasta factory in the East Bay.

I *feel* you, San Francisco. I can hear you buzzing in my ear like a honeybee, humming your site-specific tune in my head. It's eerie, melodic, jaunty, and dolorous all in one. Layered in your city sounds are tickling ivories, a low bassoon, a bossa nova beat, and strings. There's that one part with the children's choir singing, "You can't always get what you want," a harpsichord, a dulcimer, and glockenspiels played by those St. Mary's Chinese girls with the pom-pommed headdresses and silk cheongsams. A harmonica is joined by a kazoo and a Good & Plenty box. There are spoons dragged across an old-fashioned washboard, accompanied by a slide guitar and violins. There are even drums from Hippie Hill, foghorns, and always, the backbeat of the Pacific Ocean crashing against Seal Rock, and a familiar, haunting wail by the Mermen.

That's how SF sounded that Christmas night. I could hear the city in my head, between my ears as I drifted off to sleep above Haight Street, near the rainbow flag, just across Twin Peaks, on the sternum of the Indian Maiden.

33

Scrambling Past the Dahlias

The next day, Rolf, Lucy, and I decided to extend our visit, so along with my parents, we took a drive to the town where my dad was born—Watsonville, California. I wanted to visit my relatives there and to see the old house in which my dad grew up, where I'd spent several summers as a kid. I wanted to find out which emotions this place might evoke that my rational brain was blocking out. I hoped for the opportunity to have some revelation about my family and my beginnings, although I was unsure what I'd find.

The trip started out with my whole family in the car, which I knew was a bad idea, but I couldn't talk my way out of it. My dad was in the driver's seat, which I suppose was fitting since he was taking us to his hometown, and he was the one who best knew the way. Rolf was in the front passenger's seat, and my mom, Lucy, and I sat in the back. We made it past San Mateo before the bickering, second-guessing, and chitchat about the 49ers started to get to me. My left butt cheek that was slanted sideways in the cramped backseat of the Honda began to spasm. With steadily increasing volume, my mom bragged about yet another family friend's kid whom I didn't know. I desperately pressed the button to open the window for some air, but my dad had the child safety mechanism in place.

"I need to open the window!"

"What for?"

"Because I need air."

"I'll just turn on the vent."

"Can you please just press the button that unlocks the back window?"

"Hold on. The vent is on low. Can you feel it?"

"No. Can I please just open the window?"

"I'll turn the vent on medium."

"Please just let me open the window."

"You'll feel the vent any second."

Sweltering and breathing recirculated air, I reverted, once again, to pretending I was dead. The sound track to my life-long passive captivity was the same as it ever was, Mathis and Sinatra. I didn't care for this music, but to my parents the songs were just so good. Timeless. As our separate energies shifted and settled down to their lowest common denominator, my mom changed the subject of conversation to *Dancing with the Stars*, while I continued my corpse-in-the-car routine. I embodied the collective soul sickness of adult children in backseats everywhere. There was no escape. And I knew it. We all knew it. The steamy aroma of to-go dim sum packed into Styrofoam containers next to my feet permeated the locked-window interior. My parents bickered over who was the best dancer last night. Rolf stared out the window, and Lucy wailed that she was sooooo bored. She began to kick in her seat. Oh, how peaceful it was to be dead.

After a while I couldn't take it. Lucy was becoming further agitated, so I dug around in my bag for a stuffed animal. I only had one, and it was a "Honker" from *Sesame Street*, which is a lesser-known category of Muppet who communicates only by honking his bulbous orange nose or tooting the little horns next to his ears.

"Here, take him," I said to Lucy.

She stopped kicking and hugged the Honker.

"What's his name?"

"Honky!"

I stifled a laugh, and said, "Um, maybe we can think of another name."

She thought for a moment. "Horny?"

"Uh . . ."

"I like both names. Do I have to choose?"

"No, you don't have to choose. Call him what you like."

"All right. I'll just call him Horny Honky."

When we finally arrived at the house, we were greeted by my aunt and cousin. They led us up through the front yard, and as I walked the path, I remembered an old photo I once saw of my grandma Ruby, posing on the front steps in a squirrel-collared jacket and smart chapeau. Her clothes were fancy, but her eyes were sad. The picture must have been taken in the late 1920s. This stucco dwelling had been the only two-story house on the block back then, built with money from a gambling business.

Men had come from all around to play card games and dice, and they would sometimes stay to take their meals or buy tickets for the Chinese lottery.

This was the house where my dad grew up with only one pair of shoes until he was six years old, where they played out back in the garden and sometimes walked to the end of the block and waded in the Pajaro River. There were relatives and nonrelatives around, all called "Uncle," or "Auntie." There were adopted girls like Ah Foon, a seventeen-year-old who died of scarlet fever. I knew these details just from word-of-mouth stories. From the outside, the house looked like an ordinary building. I tried to hold all these details in my head as I walked from the porch through the front door.

Once inside, I remembered the old piano that had once stood against the back wall, and the yellow-painted kitchen with tongue-and-groove wainscoting. The kitchen was now remodeled, with a center island and pretty window boxes for orchids. As I stood there taking notice of the modern appliances, all I could think of was the old kitchen where I'd sat on the linoleum floor as a kid and played with the gigantic Siamese cat whose name was Big, which was short for Big City Kitty. In fact, there had been several cats in succession called Big, all named after the first one. After all the Bigs, there were other cats, all named Boy. How pathetic it was that I apparently knew more about the lineage of the pets than that of my family. I washed my hands and helped set out the dim sum we'd brought.

As everyone talked and mingled, I made sure Lucy had something to drink and then wandered down the hall and peeked into my cousin Craig's room. In the 1970s, I had been so intimidated by my older cousin. On the walls he'd had Bruce Lee and Farrah Fawcett posters, and a hook rug emblazoned with the image of Fonzie from *Happy Days*. He used to listen to "Cat Scratch Fever" and would be holed up in his room with his friend Morgan, who was a dead ringer for Luke Skywalker. It had all seemed so glamorous and grown up to me then, and now here I was, staring into the same room, newly decorated and missing all traces of my dad's 1940s childhood as well as my 1970s memories.

Out on the landing of the back stairs, where once was just a concrete slab, there now was an extended deck with a fancy Jacuzzi. Craig was showing Lucy how to play Angry Birds on his phone. They were laughing hysterically as the bombs exploded on the piggies. Lucy had never seen anything like this game because we've deprived her of electronic media, and Craig was obviously delighted that she was so easily entertained.

My aunt led us out to the back garden and gave us a tour of the different flowers and vegetables she was growing.

"I remember my mom grew everything here," she said. As I walked through the rows of different kinds of squash and cabbage, the tomato plants, and the peach trees, I could easily imagine a stooped-over, old Chinese woman tending to her winter melons. My aunt's mother had passed away long before I started spending summers here, but her spirit seemed to linger still in this garden. In the hot sunlight, I inhaled the dusty smell of heated concrete, jasmine, and the faint decay of the giant sunflowers so tall with their bowed heads that they flopped over at the weakest point of their thin, shriveled necks. The dying blossoms, which must have been glorious blooms just a few weeks ago, were now like mournful showerheads slumped in shame, with pain, or in deference. A Chinese deference, it seemed to me.

Was this really the same plot of land where I had once fled in terror as I was chased by my brothers and cousins who shot at me mercilessly with their tracer guns? The hard plastic discs the size of pennies hit with rapidity and precision. The only thought in my six-year-old head had been, *RUN!* Back then, if my Chinese ancestors had been ghosts in the garden watching me, I'm sure they would have been amused by my roly-poly body scrambling past the dahlias, running for my life in tube socks and knock-off Adidas. As if. As if that little butterball would grow up to be the teller of their tales. Maybe as they hovered invisibly in the patch of carrots they had pity on me and said to one another, "All right. Let's trip up these boys chasing her. Let that piglet make it to the back stairs and into the house. There she can hide beneath her mama's legs under the mah-jongg table."

That was more than three decades ago, and I did make it unscathed into the house, having been spared by the wannabe Stormtroopers with plastic guns. In contrast to that day of anguish, this afternoon was peaceful and happy. Craig and Lucy continued to enjoy each other's company with their electronic mediator, my parents and aunt had a good time talking, and Rolf and I hit the Ping-Pong ball back and forth on the table in the back driveway. No one talked about unpleasant topics, and I managed not to say anything that might upset anyone.

I didn't ask about the Chinese restaurant down the street that allegedly had a machine gun mounted on the roof, and I didn't say, "Is it really true that a prostitute was Uncle Vincent's babysitter?"

We all ate dim sum and fruit salad and had hot tea afterward. We made polite conversation. I sifted through my portion of fruit and found all the pitted cherry halves to give to Lucy, who chewed them with gusto.

But I wanted to ask so many things. I wanted to ask about

unwanted pregnancies, girls who were given away, babies that died, and twin sisters separated as children. But I couldn't. The house was pretty and remodeled. The trash heap was now a fancy Jacuzzi. The patchy front yard was now an amazing oasis of lovingly pruned miniature maple trees, manzanita, and exotic flowers. Nor did the electronic blips and bleeps of Angry Birds lend itself to asking invasive family questions. I told myself, *Don't make trouble.*

I wanted to know so many things, but I couldn't conjure any reason why specific details were really any of my business. Did I need to know the exact truth about everything? Maybe I could just accept that the Chinese past was studded with hardships and leave it at that. Was it really necessary to dig up the bodies and extract the gold fillings from dead people's molars?

Of course not. I wouldn't rock the boat. I didn't want to be impolite, but as I sat there sipping my tea it occurred to me that it was moments like these that accounted for why so many Chinese Americans don't know anything about their own history. I see plenty of us around looking modern and clueless at the shopping mall, and I wonder how many other people's parents are shielding them from their own family histories. The old folks may hope to keep us from suffering, but as a result, now they've got to suffer fools. And *we* are those fools!

Elders, tell us what you know so that we can understand where we came from, and where you've been to get us where we are now. We can't stand tall on a puffy, cotton candy cloud. No matter how sweet it tastes to be sitting pretty now, we can't seem to ever get our footing. The ground evaporates beneath us because our families have wanted to save us pain. But really, we need to know.

We Chinese Americans are walking around in our modern

lives, but who and what are we carrying around, invisibly, inside us?

I am always thinking about how pursuing the life I want is a privilege. My stairs to climb are the backs of my uncles, aunts, and cousins who didn't get so far. They didn't have the time, chutzpah, luck, or stupid optimism to fall in love, have a baby, or pursue their illogical dreams. Is that for better or worse? Maybe worse for them, and better for me? They weren't cheeky enough to want for themselves. Or were they stomped down?

How did I get to slip by? Was no one watching, or were they playing interference so I could rush by? Did I lunge forward through the closing door—like a selfish jerk—or were they holding the gate open for me? Or did I just miss getting tripped by a relative's outstretched foot? I'm lucky, I know. Whose stories do I tell first? And how do I tell them if no one will share what they know?

Over the years I have thought about this Watsonville house a lot, and of all the relatives who may have once slept here but then scattered across the country as time went on. I wondered about the day-to-day activities, the sibling dynamics, rivalries, loves, and jealousies that took place in these rooms. As I went about my life, I could only imagine those who came before me. Even as I was shopping for the hundredth time at Anthropologie at the Village of the Damned at Corte Madera, I wondered about the past. My physical body was trawling through the mall, shopping for cutie-cute housewares, but my mind often came back to my fascination with this humble place of beginning. Even as I was noticing the pretty fashion aprons, I just might have been thinking of my grandma Ruby as a young woman, wearing her apron of calico cotton that had been washed so many times the print had faded to near invisible.

I've wondered about this Watsonville house at random times. Once, at West Portal Playground in San Francisco, as I watched my daughter, I noticed that none of the moms, myself included, had had time to bother with makeup. Everyone looked so bedraggled. The weariness around the eyes was its own wild, feral eye shadow of sleeplessness, anxiety, and boredom all rolled into one. We in the kid club had washed so many bottles and done so many loads of laundry that our once supple hands now made a different sound when we picked up paper cups. The sound was that of paper against paper. It struck me as a Dust Bowl dryness, even in the fog and the rain. And for some reason that sound of papery hands rubbing together reminded me of my Watsonville forebears. I knew that my lined hands were nothing compared to those of my relatives who had picked vegetables, washed clothes, dried fish, and did everything else under the sun without the benefit of Playtex gloves and emollient lotions.

Later, as I was driving home from the playground with my kid strapped into her car seat, I was still thinking of the hardships endured by my grandma Ruby, and how she made do during tough times in Watsonville. My reverie, though, was interrupted by the urgent knowledge that I really had to get back home in time to bid on something on eBay.

Actually, first I had to call the bank and confirm that I had enough money in my personal checking account so that my next purchase wouldn't hurl us head over heels into bankruptcy. We raced home, and once I got through the phone prompts, I was embarrassed to hear the recorded Bank of America fembot impassively recount my debits on the telephone:

"Press two for more history transactions . . . $62.40 PayPal . . . $146.50 PayPal . . . $89.68 PayPal . . . $298.08 PayPal . . ."

The perky cyborg's voice was like a stuck recording. Obviously, PayPal was my morphine clicker. It was so easy to spend the money when I couldn't see or feel the cash being sucked out of my grimy little fist. But I knew my eBay life was getting out of hand. Even as I experienced the fleeting, triumphant shudder of outbidding someone for a famille rose chafing dish, I was fairly certain there was more to living than tapping that computer mouse like it was a giant plastic clitoris.

But back to Watsonville. As I sat in the old house for real on that day, everything was clean and pretty as I looked around. It looked as though a designer apron from Anthropologie wouldn't seem out of place there now. The advertising slogan popped into my head, "We've come a long way, baby!"

And yet. My relatives and I sat together, not saying anything. I felt a calm in the space between us, even while I imagined sadness seeping up from the floorboards. Some dead and gone memories were not mine to exhume.

Afterward, we all piled back in the car. Once more, I pretended I was a corpse in the backseat. This time, though, my dad blasted the air conditioner, either because he just happened to figure out how the dials worked, or he was trying to show consideration for my temperature preference. The car's interior quickly became too cold, but I didn't want to lobby for further adjustment for my own sake. I closed my eyes and tried to sleep. A few minutes later, I could feel Lucy's hands inside my clothes.

"What are you doing?" I asked.

"My honker is cold," she said. "Horny Honky needs to sleep in your underpants!"

She lifted the hem of my skirt and crammed her toy into the elastic of my underwear. Fine. We sped home in our sedan, away from the hot, dusty town of my dad's humble beginnings.

What had earlier felt like a cramped backseat filled with bickering and stifled freedom now struck me as a seat of relative comfort. There was a chill in the air and a Horny Honky in my underpants, but all was pretty good in my world at that moment.

34

Place Your Hand in the Beast's Mouth

Tiger Babies, let's talk about you.

I started writing this to feel closer to you. I imagine your shallow breathing as you decide whether to go to bed or to get some work done. I wonder what you are thinking now, or on any Thursday night at ten thirty. What do your eyes look like as they read, or as they rest, asleep in your head? Are you talking to someone, or thinking about your weekend errands?

When I see other Asian Americans, sometimes I feel like we are in an impossible situation. Even if we say hello or have a brief transaction in a store or business, we will never really get to know each other, and yet I feel a kinship that I want to acknowledge.

Maybe there are too many people around, watching and listening, for me to feel comfortable. I try not to look directly at you, but I'm sure my eyes show everything. And you. Your eyes give you away, too. I know I shouldn't say that, but look at us. Probably no one else can tell. But you know it. And I know it. Our Asianness is a common thing between us, maybe the only thing, but it's really obvious. We don't know if we should acknowledge it, or if that would be embarrassing.

After I go home, I wonder what you think when you're alone. Are other Asian Americans consciously thinking about their place in the world as I am? To some extent, everyone must be constantly thinking and scheming, right? We are each Brian Wilson from the Beach Boys singing "In My Room." I wonder what it would be like to be with you and listen to your tattered, long-playing record, your *Pet Sounds*.

But we talk about the weather, don't we? Current events are a-okay, but really, who the hell cares when everything alive between us goes unsaid?

We were raised by Tiger Parents, but maybe we are a different type of tiger. Biding our time on the atoll of the swampy mangrove forest, we remain motionless. We are not exactly cavorting with cobras, but we see them swimming in the muddy river water and feel them slithering beneath our forepaws. We live in the wild but conserve energy and stay alive. We hold our heads high as we navigate the water, even as the leeches try to penetrate our fur.

We, the Asian Americans who still have feelings in our veins, who dare to be vulnerable, we are somehow invisible to the world. We are tigers, too, and just as endangered.

People like us, we wind up dead because we feel too much, and hurt too much. We're not tough. That's why we often just wander deeper into the forest, never to be counted again.

But our numbers do exist. This weary species of tiger is ev-everywhere, just hiding. If you were to stand in the moonlight, after your eyes adjusted to the dimness, you might see that we are here. Our eyes are glittering in the darkness, if you would only see us.

35

Do My Dreaming and
My Scheming, Laugh at Yesterday

Who are we when no one is looking? What are we squirreling away in our hope chests? Is your heart breaking for a first kiss of inspiration? We tend to the needs of the body, to its inconvenient desires and functions, but contained inside our flesh is an invisible part of us that is too shy to demand attention but needs care and waits for us to look inward. Your inner self sits against the underside of your skin like a Chinese wallflower waiting to be asked to dance. She's got glasses and skinned knees. Every night until you acknowledge her is yet another midnight crying in the bathtub.

Maybe we are all hiding in plain sight, even from ourselves.

As for me, in Nevada City I walk around at dusk because sometimes it seems impossible that any real thinking can happen in daylight. Sometimes ideas can only come under cover of darkness. I keep moving, hoping to discover what the early evening can show me.

Wherever I go, my Chinese Americanness goes with me. If I've had the kind of day where I was out talking to a lot of people, I often need an evening walk to clear my thoughts. Being in the open air helps me to reach into that locked box, into that heart-shaped cage. Around my neck is the skeleton key, one that was made to look antique, but really is just vintage 1969.

There's a small notebook for writing stuff down tucked under my left arm. I need my right arm to do other things, like press my finger to green velvet moss growing under a cast-iron fence or touch that dewy camellia petal on a blooming tree.

Oh, there you are, Reader. I see the light on where you live. Maybe I see your silhouette near the stained-glass lampshade, or maybe you're there making dinner. Sometimes you're right near the window as night is falling. Meanwhile, I'm strolling by and I'm peeking through the pages of my notebook. Out of the corner of my eye I see the light blue of you. Through-out the neighborhood, a Morse code of kitchen lights and table lamps click on in the houses as the sky gradually dims. The air here smells fragrant with night-blooming daphne and holds the heavy electricity of impending rain.

A little farther and it's really getting dark now. I pass a cluster of white roses lit only by the streetlight, and it's eerily quiet. At an abandoned construction site is an old iron safe, cracked wide open with its door hanging off its hinges, and the only sound around is its faint creaking. No people are in sight as I turn the corner, but in this hour of darkness I can feel the eyes of hiding pets watching me.

Cutting over to Broad Street, I pass a store window that bears the name of a famous, petite street in my old hometown. It gets me to thinking about San Francisco, yet again, and I imagine the whole city paved with books like cobblestones on Maiden Lane.

I thought I knew what I was doing, moving to an area where the downtown is illuminated at night by gaslight. I thought it could show me something about the past, especially about my own past that perhaps I couldn't see from where I was standing in San Francisco. However, for all these months in Nevada City, some feeling of home should be humming through me by now, but I'm still waiting for it.

I hear laughter and duck down a darkened street. I'm still so forever citified that I make a mental note that I have sturdy shoes on, just in case I have to run from the Zodiac killer or an insane pit bull. I've got my ballpoint pen in my hand in case I've got to spontaneously jab it at a would-be attacker. Get any closer and this hardbound notebook could be lodged up against your Adam's apple. Go ahead and try it. At this moment I want one stereotype to be true: that all Chinese people are taught kung fu at birth. Don't make me get all Bruce Lee on your ass.

Forgive me. I really don't mean to be so suspicious. It's just that I was raised in the city—a loving, hardscrabble city, surrounded by water and clouds, a moody sky and scarred souls. And in this new place I've got nowhere to conceal myself. When it starts to drizzle, I remember that now I've got no San Francisco Public Library in which to hide on rainy days. I miss the creaking chairs and library smells and going up to look at the old, black-bound city directories from the 1870s. I could also flip through the phone books from the 1940s and see my grandmother's phone number from back then, or look up her old address on Stockton Street before the Broadway Tunnel was built. It was soothing to know that the San Francisco Main Library held these catacombs of information for all the Chinese people who came early to San Francisco and were brave enough to allow themselves to be counted in the census. They are long gone by now, but I can still see their names in black on the faded white pages of the old city directories.

We will never know the names of many Chinese settlers, or who they were. They, too, lived in the in-between time. They came on ships and lived temporarily in the hulls of those vessels, between China and America. Arriving just short of the North American continent, they were then detained in barracks on Angel Island, waiting for their turn to be called to see if they'd be allowed to travel the short distance to San Francisco. If they passed their interrogation, maybe they moved to Chinatown and lived in the alleyways between charred buildings rebuilt several times over the decades. Those early Chinese were often between jobs, between towns, between generations, and between worlds. There may be no remnants left of their existence, no names in books, but as I used to walk through the city, their joys and unspoken desires seeped up through the dirt and concrete and into the soles of my feet like a voodoo powder that electrified me.

In San Francisco, I felt a comfort in strolling the sidewalks where a Chinese person a hundred years ago would have feared to tread. Even in my dad's youth, he said he never liked to leave Chinatown because he knew he'd be fair game for a pummeling if he crossed any of the invisible borders past Powell Street or Kearny, Bush Street or Broadway.

These threads of city life still string me along as I go about living in my new town. Oh, tonight I'm missing you again, San Francisco. I'm missing the lapping waves against the concrete right there at the Embarcadero. I'm longing for that particular cornflower blue at twilight, with squawking parrots careening overhead, as if they don't really know how to fly, like they're just making it up as they go along.

This very evening, I can picture Upper Grant Avenue, where time must be standing still as the fragrance of bread and cookies from the Italian bakery leavens the air with nostalgia and sympathy. Somehow that smell is San Francisco saying she remembers me, recalls me when I was nine years old and strolling by with my grandmother, running an errand to Figone Hardware for some twine to wrap Sunday's roast. That bakery-diesel-and-soy-sauce smell is North Beach blending into Chinatown, right near Victoria Pastry, where the sign says FIRENZE BY NIGHT, but the foggy sky and dank cold spell San Francisco, California.

Sure, these words are sentimental. But having one's emotions close to the surface, when did that become such a bad thing? Chinese Americans, don't swallow your feelings.

Back here in Nevada City, it's really starting to rain now. The cherry blossom petals that had burst from their bud-studded boughs just yesterday are too soon melting down to the new asphalt. The pink petal teardrops on the wet blacktop make the street look like licorice-cherry candy, or an exotic, shiny kind of peppermint bark.

As I turn and head back the way I came, my index finger is pounding out its own backbeat since earlier in the day I accidentally slammed it in the car door. My hand knows it hurts, just as my heart knows it aches, too. The nerves in the body don't lie. But they both go on, my writing hand and my silly heart, and I can feel them both pulsating as I head back toward home.

Oh wow. There. I just said it. I'm walking back to my house in Nevada City, and I just called it home.

36

Bring On the Playdates

A Tiger Mom might say, "No playdates. Absolutely not." Well, that would certainly limit the level of chaos in one's home. But as much as I enjoy a clean house, there are more important things than crumb-free countertops.

I want all my daughter's little pals to feel welcome here, and that simple desire, when broken down into details, requires more willpower, patience, and flexibility than I've ever needed to summon in school or in a paid job.

Playdates, which occur on many weekdays after school and on Saturdays, are when my daughter and her friends gleefully and unintentionally destroy our house. These afternoon sessions are by far the most difficult, ongoing tests of my mental stability, physical stamina, and psychological elasticity.

Recently, Lucy had a couple of friends over, and I had made cupcakes for them. I kept saying, "Eat over your bowl," and

"Don't drop any crumbs," but without exception, each one, at some point, accidentally dumped her bowlful of crumbs either all over herself or sent it skittering across the floor. I was fit to be tied. Moments before, the kitchen had been perfect. I had just finished cleaning because we were having a dinner party that same night. I had spent the whole morning cooking and straightening up, and now that crumbs had rained down everywhere like ant-attracting confetti, I was ready to pitch a fit. You have no idea how much I wanted to scream, "Didn't I just warn you about that?" or "What the f*ck!"

But instead, I said, "Are you okay?"

I have noticed that in moments like these, there is always a split second when a kid looks at you, and you can just tell that in her head she is performing lightning-quick calculations as to whether or not you're gonna go Captain Insane-O on her. A wide-eyed stare, panicked facial expression, or barely perceptible flinch signals that she is ready for the worst-case scenario, your anger. If you blow your stack, trust pops like a bubble.

Of course, sometimes a kid does that one thing you said not to do *on purpose*. I've witnessed a kid pick up his drink, make sure I was watching, and calmly and evilly turn over his cup so that the milk I just poured went splashing across the table. In that instance, he really deserved a well-timed, scathing expletive aimed his way. However, bellowing at piglets, petulant or just clumsy, doesn't help anyone.

In any case, after I swept up the cupcake messes, my daughter and one of her friends ran upstairs to play, and I stayed downstairs with the other pal, and we watched a Harry Potter movie together.

Now this girl was a very big fan of this series and had already seen all the movies several times. She wielded the pause and fast-forward buttons of the remote control with her nimble fingers so quickly that the film went by in staggered snippets that were impossible to track with the human eye. But she was so excited to tell me every detail of every article of clothing, set design, green screen technological moment, and plot deviation that I was forced to adjust my mentality to the level of an eleven-year-old girl's brain soaked in soda and sprinkled liberally with Pixy Stix.

It was okay. I could've fought with her but instead I told myself, *Feel the force of the brain scramble flowing through you.* I recalibrated myself to chatterbox light speed. Simultaneously, I ate some potato chips to distract myself from the thumping, crashing noises that were coming from upstairs.

People! This is what living with children is like.

After a while, I went upstairs to see what Lucy and her friend were up to. The carpet was littered with shredded toilet paper (clean) and tiny toy parts. Disassembled, minuscule bits of Japanese erasers were scattered everywhere. Also, a giant bucket of plastic Perler beads had been dumped and mashed into the carpet pile, and various stuffed animals, books, and other detritus of childhood had exploded across the beds and every square foot of the floor.

I stood there and winced in pain at the sight. As I collected my thoughts, all I said was, "Okaaaay."

I couldn't imagine how I or we were ever going to put everything back in order, but in those few moments in which I paused, I could see that they were in the middle of creating their own movie that they had carefully written and staged. They had a script, had set up all the scenes, and were now filming with the video setting of our digital camera. It was called

Evil Taco's Revenge! and starred a rather funny-looking, stuffed chinchilla named Chacho in a main role as a devious caterer.

How could I put a stop to such a thing? I couldn't—and wouldn't!

In the course of their elaborate play, these two cherubs had upended every container of toys, socks, pens, paper, and knick-knacks in sight. Everything was mashed together in the scattered wake of their destruction. What had taken me five hours to clean that morning had been obliterated by them in twenty minutes.

It took all my strength not to lose my mind. I could feel the imaginary steam ready to blow out my ears like in a cartoon.

And yet. I stopped myself. I reminded myself that they were doing exactly what children should be doing. This freedom to play as children would influence them for the rest of their lives and would lay the foundation for all their future work as adults. This inventive play was expanding the crevices of their mind, like the universe expands, creating new spiral galaxies where once there was only black nothingness.

I resisted with all my might the urge to scream. Besides, in deep space, no one can hear you anyway.

The chaos was not entirely destruction, but creation. They had literally made a holy mess. The chaos was a result of their sacred play.

Spills can be cleaned. Rugs can be vacuumed and sheets washed. Sure I want a clean home, and I would love it if clothes that I folded an hour ago actually stayed in a neat pile.

But look! How could I argue with their excitement and pure focus as they carefully measured out their screen shots and exclaimed, "Turn Chacho to the left! Okay, wait . . . chain him up in Mardi Gras beads! Now roll out the toilet paper . . ." and so forth.

I left them alone. These nine-year-olds were creating new worlds. These worlds were portals to their future, and their dreams. This imaginative play was their work. And they were creating a wonderful, lively, brilliant universe along with their mess.

And in the mix, eventually math homework still got done. Top grades were still achieved. I did clean a little more, but it was worth it to allow them their freedom. I mean, how many years left do children have to explore the far reaches of their nonsensical, quirky, malleable minds? Of course, hopefully, that creativity would never stop, even far into adulthood. That would be the most beautiful ability of all, to always have hearts and minds bursting with exuberant ideas. If only all our years could continue to be filled with that kind of self-generating happiness and wonderment. By allowing kids to play uninter-rupted, if we can give our kids the gift of never feeling stuck in life, well, dang, we all deserve that.

37

Friends Don't Let Friends Be Tiger Moms

Now that I've ventured out from my separate cage, I've found female friends who can be described as neither Tiger Moms nor cougars. All are hardworking women, and each maintains her own independence in the face of balancing professional and domestic lives, personhood and motherhood. Any one of these remarkable women would lift a freaking car off my child if need be. And they would gently send me home if they ever found me in public wearing head-to-toe nonironic leopard print.

If I were a Tiger Mom, I don't think I'd ever have gotten close enough to these friends to know that we all deal with the same challenges every day. We are each doing all that needs to be done: lugging tons of heavy backpacks and groceries, making breakfasts and packing lunches, helping with homework, and coordinating multiple schedules. Someone is always jostling our bodies, ripping open the shower curtain to talk to us, pilfering that special snack we were saving in the fridge, or crashing our computers with games and "inappropriate" movies.

Resisting the Tigerish tendency to think I can do everything all on my own has been a years-long process. I am proud to say that I don't feel in competition with my other mother-friends. I feel cooperative.

But this trust did not happen immediately. Because I hadn't had a lot of experience with close relationships up to this point, and had mostly just confined myself to my isolating Chinese box, I wasn't quite sure how to go about feeling comfortable with a new group of friends. And even when I was giving lavish, weekly dinner parties and had stepped over the line to the Dark Side of Perfect Wife, I was still using that posture as dazzle camouflage. I may have looked like I was inviting people in, even as I was simultaneously keeping them at arm's length.

Without being too conscious of it, I must have been figuring that I would only show people what I wanted them to see. If I then ended up getting hurt, I could take solace in the fact that they never knew the real me.

It was as if my insides were constructed like the *Titanic*. The ship consisted of five compartments that could fill up with water, and if the hull took a direct hit and one part filled up, the other four were still intact to keep the vessel afloat. The engineering strategy was to avoid a huge gouge across all five sections that would result in a nonsurvivable situation like the one that sank that ill-fated ship. Letting people only see one side of me was like filling up just one quadrant of my heart. If moving here and making these friends turned out to be an epic fail, I could still survive. At least, that was my initial thinking.

But slowly, ever so incrementally, I did allow myself to let in one friend at a time. I discovered that we are all in the same boat. We are all bailing water with Dixie cups. My friends showed me I was not alone in this endeavor, or in my loneliness. I did not have to pretend I was a perfect anything. I could be myself and feel welcome. And loved, for real.

Parenthood is like volunteering for an overnight field trip that lasts eighteen-plus years. I feel lucky to have discovered other sane adults who are my cochaperones. Boxes must be hauled, car rides must be arranged, and we are each forever picking up the slack. Figuratively, and sometimes literally, we do the heavy lifting, and we put down the hammer.

As mothers, we pick up kids, and in between driving everyone everywhere, we are also forced to pick ourselves up over and over again. We coax splinters out of soft little feet, soothe inexplicably hurt feelings, and wipe away hot tears rolling down cheeks, sometimes our very own.

We are the providers of hearth and home, even though we are making things up as we go along. But thank goodness we are not in separate cages, but instead, we slog through the trenches together.

For instance, a few of my friends and I recently took our daughters to a kid birthday party. It was at a bowling alley on a Saturday afternoon, and needless to say, none of us really wanted to go. However, we were all willing to throw ourselves under the bus for the sake of our children's happiness.

We entered the building and immediately the aroma of popcorn, French fries, and smelly feet enveloped us like a warm, toasty fart. We could hear and feel the cavernous space vibrating with 1980s music, the drone of overlapping voices on the loudspeakers, and the crying, sobbing, and screeching of toddlers and preteens all collectively hopped up on Sweet Tarts. As our daughters joined their gang, I exchanged glances with the other mothers. Each of our facial expressions was somewhere on the spectrum between slightly chagrined and completely miserable. One woman appeared particularly desperate, as if she were trying to decide if now was the right time to swallow the cyanide pill she kept in her purse for just such an occasion.

We were surrounded by germ-infested chaos. Six-year-olds with rubbery limbs and five Twizzlers simultaneously hanging out of their mouths were hoisting seven-pound bowling balls over their potentially licey heads. With all their might, they tossed them like gigantic, crashing jawbreakers across the scuffed lanes. I could feel the ground rumble beneath my feet, and when I looked across the trash-strewn floor, I noticed puddles of unidentifiable liquid that hadn't been cleaned up in who knows how long.

A bowling alley employee assigned to facilitate the party tried to perk up the morose birthday girl by asking, "Are you excited? Are you SUPER DUPER EXCITED?" The birthday girl looked near tears and just nodded mutely.

Just then I witnessed a bowling ball catapulted haphazardly into a gaggle of kids, barely missing someone's cherubic, mullet-framed face. Aghast at the mayhem all around us, I turned to the employee and said, "Are you insured? Are you SUPER DUPER INSURED?"

I watched Lucy from a respectable distance. I was not quite a helicopter mom, but more like a crop duster flying low in the near distance. I wanted to give my daughter space to interact with her pals without me, and to let her navigate her own needs. It was satisfying to see her not freak out when she ended up with fruit punch instead of pink lemonade, and she waited her turn politely and didn't stomp on any little kids. She gave them some withering glances, but she kept her hands and thoughts to herself, which seemed pretty good to me. I watched as she laughed with her friends, carefully rolled the ball down her lane, and did goofy victory dances when she managed to knock any pins down. She didn't look around in search of my assurances or approval, and I was proud of her independence. And best of all, she looked like she was having a good time.

We mothers shared the duties of splitting servings of French fries, divvying up the cake, and making sure kids didn't kill one another over the goody bags. All of us together pitching in to corral our little creatures really did make the experience more manageable. And when you are raising a kid, sometimes that's the best one can hope for.

After a while, a wail erupted above the din. It was a piercing, high-pitched, dental drill sound that could only be produced by the vocal cords of a human female under the age of ten. I prayed, prayed, prayed that it was not my child. I had just taken a break to eat a single French fry, and I hoped the squeal would magically go away, but it did not. It only morphed into a jackal's howl. As I glanced around, I continued to silently implore the powers that be that my child would not be the one who required assistance.

And miraculously, it wasn't my daughter who was pitching the fit. I spotted Lucy rolling a bowling ball down one of the lanes and was relieved. But then, the screeching continued. I scanned the area and spotted the piglet in peril. It was my friend's youngest daughter, and she had wiped out in one of the lanes and had dropped her drink.

I scrambled over to her and helped her up.

"Hey, it's okay," I said.

I cleaned her off as best as I could with some Kleenex from my pocket, sopped up her drink with a wad of napkins, and then led her back over to the rest of the party. Her braying stopped and downshifted to a silent scream, the kind where the mouth is open so wide that you can see tonsils, but no sound comes out.

Her mother came back from the bathroom, and as soon as the kid spotted her, the screech that erupted from the thirty-pound body was louder than any of the previous noises. It was like she had just been resting her lungs for a bit, but now that she had spotted her mom, she resumed her siren's wail.

"I think she's okay," I said, handing over the disheveled kid.

"Oh, Lordy," my friend replied, scooping up her daughter. "Thanks."

"No problem."

If that had actually been Lucy who was crying, and if I had been temporarily not around, I am certain that one of my friends would have comforted her in my absence. I know that Stephanie, or Jo, or Carol, or Kathryn, or Julie would have been there. We are all mothers. We have all been there and will be there again when it is our child who needs help, whether we need a hand or lend a hand.

And if any of us were Tiger Mothers, chances are we wouldn't have even been together at this crazy party. Maybe if we had stayed home and not allowed our kids to come, we could have counted on that Saturday afternoon being quieter and calmer. None of this chaos would have invaded our lives. However, this is life. Life is ketchup on your clothes, French fries in your hair, and cake mashed around your kid's mouth.

When we were all leaving the bowling alley, I offered my friend's kid some Reese's Pieces but accidentally said "Reese's Penis."

I was mortified. But that's life, too. When I'm frazzled, the part of my mind that always has one foot in the gutter has a tendency to trip me up. Oh, well! I told the kid's mother what I'd said, and we had a good laugh about it.

And we laughed all the way home. We know that these ridiculous, embarrassing, nerve-singeing details are all part of this giant ball of string we are rolling up a hill, together. But we've got our eye on the prize: a happy, varied, all-inclusive life experience made better with friends for our children, and friends for adults as well.

Our families are not just our biological ones, but the ones we make, too.

38

The Reamer Can't Hide the Pride

My own mother, Irene, may have kind of ignored me, and she wasn't very physically demonstrative, but she never clipped my wings so I wouldn't fly. My mom is a master, or mistress, of telling it like it is. She is blunt to the core and would never hesitate to say something looked cheap, was overpriced, tasted bad, or was just plain terrible. She never spared feelings. Like I said earlier, instead of Irene, she is sometimes called I Ream, or just the Reamer.

As I get older I am beginning to see that my mother's adherence to practicality above all else served a specific goal. The Reamer did not push me toward accomplishment solely to reflect well on her. As her child, I was to her not merely an extension of herself, whose only purpose was to serve in exalting her. I can see now that our relationship was forged with the goal of my independence. The Reamer did not coddle me. But it wasn't for lack of love. She did not coddle me *because* she loved me. She wanted me to be strong so I could live without her.

These days my mother says she raised me to be my own person. Does that mean she willingly gave me the tools to chip away at the foundation that bolted me to her? Does it mean she didn't let me hug her too much *on purpose* so I wouldn't get too attached and be afraid to break free?

Well, we could all say we did something on purpose in retrospect; that is, if everything actually worked out, which it did. I think the Reamer was just not naturally too snuggly and was simply not overendowed with sentimentality. Plus, she was busy, and didn't realize how short the window would be, the window of time in which we could feel intimate with each other. That window was narrow, indeed. Who knew it could slam shut so fast? And the tiny, mangled hand of my tender heart that got caught in the hastily slammed frame took a long time to heal.

I've forgiven my mom for her natural stoicism, her fears for me, and the projection of her own worries. She worked hard and did the best she could. She wanted good things for me, and a good life. And I think she accepts that I had to fly a short distance away from her because her love pecks, from my point of view, felt instead like sharp pluckings of my pinfeathers that would've hindered flight sooner or later.

As with many families, I think as mother and daughter we're a little closer now that I've moved away. There's space to breathe, and between us is a nonmilitarized zone of years having passed. When I go back to San Francisco to visit, there is a cease-fire in the squabbling because our time together is set on a timer.

I am thankful to my parents for letting me go. I'm glad that *they* are independent, too. The upside to my mother's natural lack of sentimentality is that I'm not regularly mopping up her drunken carcass from the floor of a karaoke bar after she's belted out "Feelings." Or if she was Filipina, "Peelings."

The reality of my mom's lifelong habit of being practical and unemotional above all else means that she calls up and asks if I need anything at Costco, rather than ringing me up at midnight to rehash some hysterical argument from 2007. I've got friends whose parents do that, and I'm so glad that's not anything my mother would do. It turns out that Tiger Mom qualities have some benefits, after all. My mother still might not be very comfortable hugging me, but I know that that ninety-six-pack of toilet paper means she truly loves me.

It's a stoic kind of love, but it's love just the same. For instance, every year on my birthday, my parents send me a store-bought card, and at the bottom of the printed message, it is always signed, "From Your Family." The lettering is engineer-perfect, in all capital letters, and there is no extra "Love," or other sentimental addition to the matter-of-fact statement. There is no inclusion of the words *Mom* or *Dad*. The implied existence of my brothers, uncles, aunts, and other relatives hovers invisibly in the all-encompassing word, *Family*.

This three-word phrase says it all about Chinese thinking. This birthday card sign-off tells me everything I need to know as their daughter. Not including the individual names indicates that our specific identities are, overall, inconsequential. We are family. Also, no amount of frilly exclamations or lack thereof makes any difference either. If they adore me, hate my guts, or feel just kinda "eh" about me, the bedrock truth is that we are family. No matter what.

This year my birthday card arrived, and as expected, it was

signed in the exact same manner. Actually, my own name was not anywhere on the card either, but at the bottom, there were the usual words, *From Your Family.* The card itself had a picture of Snoopy and a wide rainbow flag across the top. When I opened the flap, the card fanned out like a pop-up book, and the big block letters read, "CAN'T HIDE THE PRIDE!"

I wasn't sure if my parents were trying to tell me that they thought I was gay. Or maybe they just remembered that when I was nine years old I liked Snoopy. Either way, I've taken the message to heart. My family, whatever their names are, are proud of me.

39

Something Rejected Is the Key to Your Heart

Strict parenting that accepts nothing less than The Best has more pitfalls than benefits, if you ask me. Chinese moms and dads might tell themselves it is their responsibility to push us as hard as we kids can take, but their austerity and inflexibility have long-term consequences. Perhaps they hide behind the platitude "This is the Chinese way" so they don't have to dwell on the fact that we feel constantly denied acceptance. But as a result of this denial of love, we might grow up so emotionally shut down that nothing good can be let into our hearts. They wanted us to toughen up, but didn't suspect we were growing scar tissue so thick to protect ourselves from our own families.

Mamas, don't let your babies grow up to be robots. With Chinese-style tough love, I actually am *not feelin' the love*. Ever.

I guess all parents want to control their kids. But maybe instead of tightening the grip around our loved ones' throats, we could take some parenting advice from the dialogue in *Star Wars*. We could remember Princess Leia saying, "The more you tighten your grip, [Governor] Tarkin, the more star systems will slip through your fingers."

Because that's what I wanted to do. Slip away. Chinese parents are like Darth Vader. They can choke you without even touching you.

For many Chinese parents, saving face is synonymous with denying us our own faces. And maybe we like Hello Kitty so much because we ourselves feel as vulnerable as Mimmy, Kitty, and Chococat look. We are wide-eyed in the face of Tiger Mom's all-encompassing power.

Didn't you see *Spider-Man*? With great power comes great responsibility. If you're going to try to squelch us, we're going to have to go underground. We will burrow out of sight with our emotions and our deepest dreams. You are projecting your unfulfilled hopes onto us, but what about our own? We're stealth now. No ship that small has a cloaking device. Yes, we're the *Millennium Falcon*. You think you are forcing us into light speed, but we are floating away from you with the cosmic trash. We'll lie dormant in the belly of a giant space worm just to get the heck away from you. Your love is an asteroid field. You are an Imperial Star Destroyer and we navigate away from you.

And we are still hiding. Maybe in your zeal to make us into walking advertisements to exalt you, you forget that Tiger Babies grow up someday. Let's get real. Who has the power? The next generation. Regardless of what you've tried to protect us from, or protect yourself from, we're going to do what we want.

And now we have babies of our own. There's the rub. Our own babies are where we draw the line. You want control of them, too, but we won't allow what happened to us to become their reality as well. We're going to believe our babies when they say they're hurt, not tell them to shut up and stop crying because tears will make them mediocre.

We are emotional beings. Our vulnerability scares you, but our continued openness is the only hope for you, Tiger Parent, reformed or not. We artists, secretaries, comic book geeks, and marginally employed individuals might be failures in your eyes. But we are the ones who don't give up on you. We are the nurturers, the snuggle bunnies. Is it so terrible to be soft? You are afraid to let our vulnerability rain all over you, but you will not reign over us any longer. Your unyielding stoicism is the problem, not our openness.

Tiger Parents, listen up. While we were sitting in detention, while we were bored in Chinese school, we were making skeleton keys from mangled paper clips. We have bent and molded this twisted, rejected piece of metal into the key to your heart. We've got other good qualities that you simply have missed. You can still love us. Catch us if you can.

Epilogue

Tiger Parents, you may be asking yourselves, "What is the point of this book?"

Love your babies, and show your babies that you love them. Withholding acceptance and praise while pushing your children into achievement might yield certain results, but that kind of pressure stifles other aspects of growing up.

Rote memorization, blind obedience, and top scores at the expense of developing passion or true understanding for a subject actually impede creativity, spontaneity, developing social skills, trust, camaraderie, and the ability to love.

And these are all things we need in life. The resulting young adult of Tiger parenting might reach the top of his or her chosen professional field, but might not have any friends. Tiger Parents, do you really want your kids to be so messed up they can't find partners or have kids of their own?

Tiger Mom, it's very simple. If you want grandkids, get off your kids' case and stop micromanaging every aspect of life.

And Tiger Babies, just for you:

Below are the *Tiger Babies Strike Back* pop quiz answers, which will definitely be on the test:

1. Have an emotional life. Even if it is only in private, take out your emotional ball of wax and roll it around in your hand. Your feelings are real. Don't tamp them down. Chinese people are taught to keep it all in, but please don't close yourself off from the world. Talk to someone. If there isn't anyone else around, talk gently to yourself. You matter.

2. Second best ain't worth killing yourself over. I will never know what might have helped my aunt who jumped off the Golden Gate Bridge. Failure as defined by other people, especially your elders, doesn't have to have absolute power over you.

3. Please yourself. Maybe nothing will ever be good enough for your parents. You might never please them no matter how hard you try, or how much you do. Do things for yourself, without their permission. Your family will have to get over it.

4. Take care of your own body. Do it for yourself. You are reason enough to eat well and look and feel good.

5. This information will not actually be on the test. There is no test. Go outside and get some fresh air instead.

About the Author

The only thing that keeps Kim Wong Keltner from writing is when she's trapped under an avalanche of her daughter's stuffed animals. Kim is the author of *The Dim Sum of All Things, Buddha Baby,* and *I Want Candy. Tiger Babies Strike Back* is her first work of nonfiction. She can be contacted at kimwongkeltner.com.

BOOKS BY KIM WONG KELTNER

TIGER BABIES STRIKE BACK
How I Was Raised by a Tiger Mom but Could Not Be Turned to the Dark Side
Available in Paperback and eBook

Sparked by the heated debate surrounding the publication of Amy Chua's *Battle Hymn of the Tiger Mother*, *Tiger Babies Strike Back* is a funny, poignant look at the real lives and challenges of women in a post-Tiger Mother world.

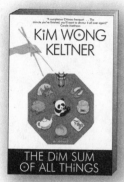

THE DIM SUM OF ALL THINGS
A Novel
Available in Paperback and eBook

"Keltner's novel is full of feisty humor . . . Smart and sassy, *Dim Sum* is a fictional feast." —*USA Today*

BUDDHA BABY
A Novel
Available in Paperback and eBook

"Wong Keltner's spunky novel . . . delivers a left hook to knee-jerk political correctness and offers a comic, honest take on what it feels like to be part of two cultures."
—*Publishers Weekly*

I WANT CANDY
A Novel
Available in Paperback and eBook

A sweet and sassy coming-of-age novel set against the backdrop of a Chinese restaurant in San Francisco.

"A smart and sassy novel about growing up Chinese American in San Francisco." —*San Francisco Chronicle*